Navigating
Implementation
OF THE
Common Core
State Standards

GETTING
READY
FOR THE
Common
Core
HANDBOOK SERIES

BOOK ONE

Navigating Implementation
OF THE
Common Core
State Standards

Douglas B. Reeves | Maryann D. Wiggs
Cathy J. Lassiter | Thomasina D. Piercy
Stephen Ventura | Bonnie Bell

LⱢP
LEAD+
LEARN
PRESS

ENGLEWOOD, COLORADO

The Leadership and Learning Center
317 Inverness Way South, Suite 150
Englewood, Colorado 80112
Phone 1.866.399.6019 | Fax 303.504.9417
www.LeadandLearn.com

Published by Lead + Learn Press, a division of Advanced Learning Centers, Inc.

Library of Congress Cataloging-in-Publication Data

Navigating implementation of the common core state standards /
Douglas B. Reeves ... [et al.].
p. cm. — (Getting ready for the common core handbook series ; bk.
One)
Includes bibliographical references and index.
ISBN 978-1-935588-14-6 (alk. paper)
1. Education—Standards—United States. I. Reeves, Douglas B., 1953-
LB3060.83.N495 2011
379.1'580973—dc23
2011034851

ISBN 978-1-935588-14-6

Printed in the United States of America

15 14 13 12 11   01 02 03 04 05 06 07

Contents

List of Exhibits

About the Authors

Douglas B. Reeves is the founder of The Leadership and Learning Center. As part of Houghton Mifflin Harcourt, a global educational leader, The Center serves school systems around the world. The author of 30 books and many articles on leadership and organizational effectiveness, Doug has twice been named to the Harvard University Distinguished Lecture Series. Doug was named the Brock International Prize laureate for his contributions to education. He also received the Distinguished Service Award from the National Association of Secondary School Principals and the Parents Choice Award for his writing for children and parents. He is the 2010 recipient of the National Staff Development Council's Contribution to the Field Award. In the foreword to Doug's 2011 book *Finding Your Leadership Focus: What Matters Most for Student Results*, Michael Fullan wrote, "Reeves doesn't just tell us what not to do. His research is so carefully documented and so clearly argued that we see precisely what should be our focus. . . . Reeves takes us further and deeper into the critical territory of whole system reform. He does it with such elegance and relentless insistence that we are drawn—indeed, compelled—to want to take action."

Maryann D. Wiggs is a Professional Development Associate with The Leadership and Learning Center. With more than four decades of experience in education, Maryann brings an abundance of expertise and wisdom to her presentations, ensuring that teachers and administrators gain practical strategies for enhancing instructional performance. As the former Assistant Superintendent of Curriculum and Instruction and Executive Director of Learning Services in two Colorado school districts, Maryann has been instrumental in orchestrating the alignment of all aspects of the leaders' and teachers' work to improve the quality of instruction in the classroom, including alignment of standards, assessment, curriculum, instruction, interventions, supervision, and evaluation. Maryann is a former speech pathologist, special and general education teacher, behavior consultant, and teacher leader, having served learners at the elementary, middle, high school, and college levels.

Cathy J. Lassiter is a Professional Development Associate with The Leadership and Learning Center. She brings a sense of passion and energy to her work on school leadership, data, curriculum, instruction, and the Common Core State Standards. She has worked with superintendents, state departments of education, school boards, principals, and teachers to improve leadership and instructional practices across the United States, Canada, and Bermuda. Over the course of her 28 years in public urban education, she was a middle and high school teacher, middle school principal, and central office administrator. While serving her district as the Senior Director of Curriculum, Instruction and Staff Development, the district won the prestigious Broad Prize in Urban Education in 2005. Cathy also supervised middle schools in her role as the Executive Director. Cathy earned her doctorate in Administration and Policy Studies from The George Washington University, and has also taught courses there in educational leadership.

Thomasina D. Piercy is a Professional Development Associate with The Leadership and Learning Center. She earned her Ph.D. in curriculum and instruction with a focus on reading from the University of Maryland. As a pre-K–12 district literacy leader, principal, and teacher, she taught graduate writing and reading courses to educators from various states in the East Coast region. Thommie's research received the Reading Research Award from the State of Maryland International Reading Association Council. She was honored with the Joseph R. Bailer Award from McDaniel College in Maryland for her distinguished career in education, and she was the recipient of the Court Appointed Special Advocates for Children Hero Award. As a teacher, she was named one of five expert teachers by the Maryland State Department of Education.

Stephen Ventura is a Professional Development Associate with The Leadership and Learning Center. He is a highly motivational and knowledgeable speaker who approaches high-stakes data collection and decision making armed with practical, research-based strategies. Steve is a former elementary, middle school, and high school teacher. His administrative experiences include serving as assistant principal, principal, director, and superintendent. Through his own reality-based experiences, Steve has inspired teachers and leaders across the nation to pursue higher levels of implementation with greater focus, rigor, and clarity. In addition to his professional development work with teachers and administrators, Steve is also a frequent speaker at local and state conferences, and has contributed to several books focused on teaching, learning, and leadership. He has a strong moral aspect, intelligence, easy way with people, and sense of humor that support him in his life and work.

Bonnie Bell is an Assistant Superintendent of Educational Services with the Claremont Unified School District in Claremont, California, and a Professional Development Associate with The Leadership and Learning Center. Her professional experience in four school districts has spanned 26 years. She has served as a classroom teacher, district mentor, categorical coordinator, county consultant, and site administrator. In addition, she has worked in diverse, academically challenging schools as well as in high socioeconomic areas. Bonnie's passion revolves around planning for systemic reform initiatives involving response to intervention, educational technology, English language learners, and academic improvement. Because of her focus on educational initiatives, schools and districts under Bonnie's leadership have been named a National Blue Ribbon School, California Distinguished School, and High Performing Title I School; have been listed on the California Business for Education Excellence Honor Roll; and have received the California School Board Association's Golden Bell award.

Introduction

Implementation of the Common Core State Standards (CCSS) provides a marvelous forum for hosting a great national conversation about what it means, explicitly, for our country's young people to be well prepared to persist in meeting the academic rigors of college and to be successful in careers spanning the globe. Widespread support of the Common Core academic standards for both English language arts and mathematics, as evidenced by the voluntary adoption of the CCSS by the vast majority of states across the country, represents an unprecedented opportunity for economies of scale toward improving the quality of education for our nation's youth. The ushering in of the CCSS in June 2010 provided educators across the United States with the opportunity to push the "refresh" button and "reboot" practices that feature a laser-like focus on rigorous English language arts and mathematics standards. The Leadership and Learning Center, founded by Douglas Reeves, has been at the forefront of implementing standards-based educational practices for nearly two decades. We invited experts from The Center to create a handbook that would serve as a "guide on the side" for educational leaders as they respond to the call to action to implement the Common Core. Each chapter anchors the reader with an understanding of the issues presented from a historical perspective, offers advice to consider in moving forward, and provides explicit step-by-step strategies to follow to successfully ramp up the best of standards-based instructional practices at all levels of the organization.

This handbook is the first in a series of four handbooks that takes a systemic approach to *Getting Ready for the Common Core.*

Handbooks, by design, are practical guides for "doing it yourself" and/or for rechecking your work and "doing over" things that can be improved upon. This handbook series effectively turns the reader's attention from the "what" to the "how"—it addresses how the CCSS should influence leadership, teaching, and learning. For nearly two decades, Douglas Reeves has challenged leaders and educators around the globe to step up to the provocative challenge of advancing student achievement for all students, while at the same time casting light on specific, replicable, research-based strategies to guide deep implementation of practices that matter most. Chapter One appropriately begins the CCSS conversation, with Douglas posing five questions that every educational leader must ask and answer in regard to making leadership decisions about the Common Core. Each of the five questions is explored and addressed.

In Chapter Two, I set the stage for getting familiar with the Common Core State Standards by providing a succinct overview that allows readers to gain perspective on the design and organizational features of the CCSS for both literacy and mathematics. Twenty strategies are provided near the end of the chapter for leading faculty and stakeholders in gaining a deeper understanding of the Common Core State Standards.

Authored by Thomasina Piercy, Chapter Three describes the historical perspective that led to the inclusion of a specific standard within the reading strand devoted to increasing the level of text complexity across K–12 schooling. This chapter is foundational in understanding the factors that contribute to why so many students are unable to access and engage with complex information. Thommie offers guidance on moving toward resolution of the issues presented.

Chapter Four deals squarely with the generalized lack of rigor found in our nation's classrooms that led to the intentional inclusion of the "higher" cognitive demand standards articulated in the CCSS. Author Cathy Lassiter provides perspective on the amount of "ramping up" that will be required of all teachers across all content areas in order to achieve the promise of the Common Core. In this handbook, educators are provided with strategies to consider in approaching the topic of "closing the rigor gap."

Chapter Five, Structures for Supporting All Learners, is included in this handbook to establish from the outset the compelling notion that the Common Core State Standards are meant for "all students, not just some students." The author, Bonnie Bell, provides explicit step-by-step strategies for supporting all students in accessing good first instruction based on the CCSS. Bonnie is direct and to the point, painting a picture of "how-to" practices that are inclusive of all students. *All standards, all students,* period.

Author Stephen Ventura provides the concluding chapter for this first volume in the *Getting Ready for the Common Core Handbook Series.* Steve provides guidance to the reader on how to design and launch an action plan for implementing the Common Core. Readers are provided with an outline of many of the benefits of designing a 100-day implementation plan, followed by details of five steps for organizing the 100-day plan. Advice on mistakes to avoid in designing a 100-day action plan, along with a graphic organizer provided by The Leadership and Learning Center, provide clear guidance for systemic alignment during the phases of planning, implementing, and monitoring the Common Core State Standards.

What's next? Each handbook in the *Getting Ready for the*

Common Core series focuses on a unifying theme to provide leaders and educators with the rationale and tools for navigating the terrain of implementing the Common Core. The second handbook provides guidance and specific strategies for navigating the English language arts CCSS, while the third handbook provides explicit suggestions for navigating the mathematics CCSS. The fourth handbook in the series focuses on using formative assessment processes and the Common Core, as well as strategies for aligning Professional Learning Communities and Data Teams practices as continuous improvement structures ensuring sustainability.

Brilliantly designed, the Common Core State Standards have become the centering force for reinvigorating challenge in our profession. The authors, validating committees, supporters, and organizers of the Common Core State Standards Initiative accomplished together what no one individual or organization could—or should—have created alone. They are to be commended for an exemplary product. It is in the spirit of leveraging expertise for implementation of our "shared" standards that The Leadership and Learning Center is pleased to provide this series of handbooks on *Getting Ready for the Common Core* to serve as a starting point for collegial conversations.

MARYANN D. WIGGS, 2011
Colorado Springs, Colorado

Leadership Decisions for the Common Core: Five Questions Every Educational Leader Must Ask ... and Answer

Douglas B. Reeves

Educational leaders face critical decisions as almost every school in the nation implements the Common Core State Standards. These leadership decisions will address the following five questions:

- **The Moral Imperative:** Why are standards the most fair and effective way to teach and assess students?

- **Preparation:** How will we meet the professional learning needs of our faculty and administrators as they prepare to implement the Common Core?

- **Monitoring:** How will system and building leaders know that the Common Core is implemented effectively?

- **Focus:** How will scarce resources of time and money be allocated to support the Common Core? What lower-priority consumers of time and money can be reduced or eliminated?

- **Balance:** Even as leadership attention is focused on student achievement of the CCSS, what *other* factors are important to our students and communities?

This chapter suggests potential answers to these questions, along with a process for collaborative inquiry and decision making for educational leaders. In addition, this chapter offers resources to which leaders can turn for additional assistance in the implementation of the Common Core.

THE MORAL IMPERATIVE: WHY STANDARDS?

Before leaders start issuing instructions and making policies about the Common Core standards, they must provide a moral framework for the implementation of standards. The justification "we have to do this in order to qualify for a federal grant" is not the compelling call to action that professionals require. Daniel Pink (2009) makes it clear that human motivation depends not upon rewards and punishments, but upon moral purpose. Teachers and school administrators spend an extraordinary amount of their time operating independently, even in an era of more frequent classroom observation and high-stakes teacher evaluation. Moreover, while administrators can compel specific behaviors of school employees, they cannot command the engagement of their hearts and minds. Students and colleagues know the difference between actions which are the result of compulsion followed by submission and actions which stem from genuine belief. Therefore, professional learning preparation for the Common Core must not begin with the premise that the Common Core State Standards are perfect—they are not. Rather, we must begin with the certain conviction that these standards, whatever their flaws, are morally superior to the bell curve. As I wrote in an *Education Week* commentary, "if you don't like standards, learn to love the bell curve" (Reeves, 2010).

Standards and Norms

There are essentially only two ways to evaluate student performance. Teachers can either compare students to one another—norm-referenced assessment—or teachers can compare students to an objective standard—standards-referenced assessment. Why is the comparison of students to each other so pernicious? After all, we have competition all the time in sports, debate, and academics. Isn't the competitive spirit what made America great? Don't we need to encourage competition among students in order to bring out their best? While I respect the depth of conviction from which these common questions arise, they conflate two distinct notions—proficiency and victory.

An exclusive emphasis on victory rather than proficiency gives us the worst of both worlds, as it renders nonproficient students complacent and suggests that proficient students are inadequate. Consider the best student in a driver's education class who, having crashed only twice during the performance exam, at least did not total the car and hospitalize the instructor as his six predecessors had done. Should this student pass with flying colors, or should all of these students be compared to appropriate standards of safe driving and all fail the test? Should they then learn from the feedback, study more, and—after a great deal more work—retake their driving tests? Conversely, if all of these students executed the required maneuvers on the driving test flawlessly, is it really essential that some must win and others must lose? In the second instance, all of the students are proficient and should receive their license. It is the same in other classes in school. The relentless search for winners and losers caused by assessment systems based on the bell curve creates distinctions among students that are not meaningful. While it should not matter to us that one student is proficient in algebra with a 98.78 average and another student is proficient in the same subject with a 98.79 average, the latter could, if that tiny distinction causes her to be the valedictorian of her school, lead her to have significantly more scholarships and higher education opportunities than the former student whose performance is not significantly different.

We can all nevertheless enjoy a good competition and we know that students enjoy it as well. But part of what makes a well-educated person is the knowledge of when to compete and when to collaborate. The bell curve makes everything—every project, every class, every interaction with a teacher, and most importantly every interaction with a classmate—competitive. While the rhetoric of 21st-century skills calls for collaboration and communication, the reality of the bell curve in the classroom is that students have no incentive to collaborate, and they will communicate only with someone who can give them a competitive edge.

Thomas Friedman (2005) notes that American students suffer from an ambition gap—that is, they simply do not work as hard as students in nations that perform better on standardized tests. While one can take issue with the use of testing as the only measure of student achievement, anyone who has lived and taught in different countries can observe the difference in the way students work (and more importantly, the way teachers are respected) in the United States compared to countries such as Finland, Singapore, Korea, and China (Darling-Hammond, 2010). American students, particularly those in the middle class and upper middle class, receive a steady diet of affirmation because they can speak, read, and write a bit better than the very large number of students in poverty and the growing number of students who are learning English as a second language. By substituting such a hollow victory for true proficiency, the students fail to challenge themselves. Only one-third of high school students write extensive research papers, and more than 70 percent of high school students admit that they are not academically challenged (Yazzie-Mintz, 2010).

PREPARATION: PROFESSIONAL LEARNING FOR THE COMMON CORE

Many readers were in schools when "standards 1.0" were introduced to schools in the 1990s. These documents, widely varying in specificity and quality (www.EdExcellence.net), were well-intentioned but often poorly executed. Hectares of trees were sacrificed as binders full of state standards documents were delivered to schoolhouse doors and then ... nothing. In many cases, classroom teaching and assessment was indistinguishable from the pre-standards era. The bell curve—comparing students to one another rather than to objective performance standards—remained the prevailing method of evaluation. Indeed, that remains the case today, with astonishing numbers of schools in which students can receive high or low grades regardless of their academic proficiency.

The Moral Imperative: Challenge the Complacent; Encourage the Discouraged

Standards-based education is a moral imperative because it demands more of students than merely beating their disadvantaged neighbors. World-class standards will challenge even our best students to work hard, respect feedback, and achieve at higher levels. At the same time, the assessment of students based on standards will encourage our most discouraged and disadvantaged students, because they are not assessed based upon the speed with which they respond to academic challenges, but rather based upon their ultimate success. Even the most disadvantaged students demonstrate success in fields as wide ranging as video games, basketball, music, art, calculus, skateboarding, and poetry, not because of their innate ability, but because of the opportunity to practice, receive feedback, and improve performance (Colvin, 2008). The simple truth is that these students have been given a standards-based approach to education in some fields, such as video games and skateboarding, where the consequence of failure is not sympathy, but virtual explosions or quite real encounters with concrete. In each of these cases, the consequence of failure is neither an "F" nor a "zero," but the immediate opportunity to pick themselves up, dust themselves off, and try again. That is the essence of standards-based education, and it is the reason that students who have the opportunity to succeed in such an environment perform remarkably better than students whose failure is sealed once they have been beaten by another student.

Although the Common Core, as with any set of standards, suffers from some deficiencies, the ultimate comparison is not between the Common Core State Standards and perfection, but between the available standards-based education and the bell curve. In every case, standards win the moral high ground. More students will succeed not based upon their inheritance, not based upon where they started the race, but based upon how they finished. That is not only better for those students, but better for the society wise enough to nurture and encourage a large number of students who succeed in meeting and exceeding standards.

How Can We Best Help Students Prepare for the Common Core?

Educational leaders must do more than ensure that Common Core standards are "delivered" to schools. They must help faculty and administrators focus on specific steps that will prepare students for the CCSS. Three essentials include identifying current curriculum and assessments that support the Common Core, significantly increasing informational writing in every discipline, and initiating a major increase in the level of mathematical rigor in almost every state.

The first step in preparation is for teachers to review the CCSS and highlight the standards that they are already teaching. This will, in most cases, relieve the anxiety of teachers who may be concerned that the Common Core represents a complete overhaul of their classroom practices. One of the most important rules of change leadership is counterintuitive, but essential: identify what does *not* change. If classroom educators perceive the underlying message that "everything I've done in the past is wrong," then resistance to the Common Core is certain. If, on the other hand, teachers perceive that they can retain their best practices that are incorporated into the Common Core and build on those time-tested practices, then faculties will proceed with collaboration rather than defensiveness. Second, leaders must commit to increasing informational writing in every discipline at every grade level. Although there is substantial research to support the value of nonfiction writing (Kiuhara, Graham, and Hawken, 2009; Reeves, 2002), the Common Core makes an emphasis on nonfiction writing particularly important. Unfortunately, the consistent use of nonfiction writing across the curriculum remains the exception rather than the rule. Many states have reduced the use of writing on their state assessments as a cost-saving move, and the unfortunate result has been the reduction of emphasis on writing in the classroom. Schools getting ready for the Common Core must make a substantial commitment to increasing informational writing at every level, starting in kindergarten. My experience is that nonfiction writing can be a fun and engaging activity for students of all ages. The Common Core research dispenses with two common arguments in schools. One argument is "I'm not a writing teacher," when, in fact, every teacher in every subject is responsible for helping students to think critically, and as author William Zinsser said, "Writing is thinking on paper." Another argument has been that writing is not "developmentally appropriate" for kindergarten students. But when kindergarten students around the world are already engaged in successful writing curricula, then it is clear that the extent to which kindergarteners write is a matter of adult expectations, not the developmental capacity of the children.

Third, teachers and administrators must examine carefully the requirements of their mathematics curriculum, as the Common Core math requirements are significantly more rigorous than many prevailing state standards. The advancement of mathematical rigor has been hampered in many schools by a combination of two factors: the abandonment of calculation at the elementary level and the resistance to mathematical modeling in middle school. There is a common argument that students don't need algebra unless they are pursuing a technical career, but schools' reluctance to require students to learn it perhaps has more to do with the fact that an alarming number of students come to high school without the mathematical skills that make advanced mathematics accessible to them. The Common Core recognizes that students need to understand the relationships among numbers (that is what algebra is all about) in order to be critical thinkers—a fundamental requirement of being a careful consumer and an educated citizen. One does not need to pursue an engineering degree to need to know a range of mathematical skills, from calculating the interest rate on a credit card to understanding the difference between different sorts of numerical progressions. Moreover, without the more rigorous mathematical curriculum requirements of the Common Core, students will never have the choice to pursue many opportunities in technical, scientific, and engineering fields.

MONITORING: HOW LEADERS CAN CHECK IMPLEMENTATION

Educational leaders cannot wait for state assessments to determine the extent to which schools are implementing the Common Core effectively. One of the most important lessons of the past two decades of the standards movement is that standards are an illusion when they are supported by only a single test at the end of the year, preceded by nine months of inconsistent curriculum and assessment based on the idiosyncratic choices of each teacher. Formative assessments—that is, assessments that are administered periodically during the school year and are designed to inform teaching and learning—can have a profound impact on student achievement (Hattie, 2009). However, assessments are not "formative" based on the label on the test, but rather based on how they are used by teachers and administrators (Popham, 2008; Ainsworth and Viegut, 2006). When teachers collaborate to create assessments based on the most essential standards, score those assessments collaboratively, and use the data from those assessments to make immediate improvements in teaching and learning, then the impact on student achievement can be dramatic (Anderson, 2010). When, on the other hand, formative assessments become a chore to be endured, after which teachers simply return to the previously planned march through the curriculum, then they can be a colossal waste of time. The value of formative assessments lies not only in the quality of the test items themselves, but also in how the information from those assessments is used. The most psychometrically elegant test is worthless without practical application by teachers.

The Challenges of Formative Assessment

One of the greatest challenges of formative assessment, however, is the common statement that students are overtested already, and that each hour devoted to testing is an hour taken away from teaching. That challenge is an appropriate one for tests that are never used by teachers to improve instruction. However, formative assessments can save time when they are used to redirect instruction, assist individual students in meeting fundamental requirements, and identify opportunities to challenge students who may become bored by a continued focus on skills and knowledge that they have already mastered. In other words, formative assessment used properly can save time for teachers and avoid costly excursions into curriculum plans that are not meeting the needs of their students.

Monitoring Causes, Not Just Effects

While formative assessment is an essential part of monitoring student progress, it is a necessary but insufficient condition for successful leadership of Common Core implementation. Teachers and administrators should establish fundamental research-based practices that can be measured, monitored, and reported so that they can analyze the relationship between teaching practices and student results. For example, they can measure the frequency of nonfiction writing activities and they can analyze the extent to which the same student work receives the same evaluation by different teachers. In addition, they can monitor the extent to which professional learning conversations lead to observable changes in teaching practices and student results.

Both What and How

While the Common Core State Standards documents are admirable in many respects, one of their weaknesses is that they suggest that the Common Core only encompasses the "what" of teaching and not the "how" (Reeves, 2010, p. 33). This is a false dichotomy, as it suggests that leaders should focus only on the content of the curriculum, rather than also assessing the manner in which it is taught. But leaders cannot, for example, insist on the inclusion of informational writing without also monitoring the most effective teaching practices associated with writing (Peery, 2011). Schools cannot monitor the implementation of the Common Core based solely on annual test scores—the primary mistake of the past decade of educational policy—but rather must continually assess adults as carefully as they assess students. The assessment of adults, it is important to note, includes leaders as well as teachers. Most importantly, assessment in this context is not the same as evaluation. Just as assessment for learning (Stiggins, Arter, Chappuis, and Chappuis, 2004) is a best practice for students, assessment for learning for adults is far more productive than annual teacher and administrator evaluations. If the purpose of assessment and monitoring is to improve the practices of teachers and leaders, then it is entirely reasonable for those monitoring activities to suggest improvements in practice. That is almost never the case with typical teacher and administrator evaluations (DuFour and Marzano, 2009; Reeves, 2008). If we expect students to improve, then they must take risks, make mistakes, and receive formative feedback that leads to improved performance. If we expect teachers and leaders to improve, then we must provide monitoring and feedback that meet the same criteria.

FOCUS: ALLOCATING SCARCE RESOURCES OF TIME AND MONEY

Schools around the nation continue to reel from the recession that began in 2008. While there are indicators of national economic recovery, the long-term effects of property devaluations and declines in tax receipts will adversely affect many school systems for years to come. This is particularly true where property taxes are the main determinant of school funding, and where elections are required to increase mill levies or sales taxes or otherwise replace lost revenue for schools. Therefore, school leaders must implement one of the most important changes in educational policy in decades with fewer economic resources. In addition, an increase in class sizes in many states (Yatvin, 2011) will cause teachers to have fewer minutes to devote to the individual needs of each student. Indeed, the greatest source of discontent for many teachers is not the lack of economic resources but the shortage of time to do their jobs effectively (Ingersoll and Perda, 2009).

Leaders therefore need a rational and publicly defensible approach to resource allocation that allows them to increase resources where necessary and make cuts in other areas without jeopardizing their essential mission. One helpful tool for leaders is the "Implementation Audit™," a process that has now been used in more than a thousand schools. The Implementation Audit addresses three questions:

- What is our initiative inventory?
- What is the range of implementation?
- What is the relationship between instructional initiatives and student achievement?

Although the questions may seem obvious, the results of Implementation Audits are surprising for many leaders. First, the inventory of instructional initiatives is almost always much more extensive than leaders perceive. A comprehensive review of school improvement plans reveals that schools, districts, and states have dozens—sometimes hundreds—of "priorities" that are never fully implemented (Reeves, 2011). Educational initiatives accumulate like layers in an ancient archeological site, with a cross section revealing one initiative stacked on top of another. There was no bad intent in the establishment of individual initiatives. Indeed, the initial allocation of resources for each one was done in good faith with the belief that the initiative would lead to improvements in student results. The problem is not the individual initiatives, but their collective impact, with each additional initiative in the school day leading to fewer minutes allowed to teachers for successful implementation.

When the data from the Implementation Audit are compiled, leaders can place instructional initiatives into the four quadrants depicted in Exhibit 1.1.

In the upper right-hand quadrant, labeled "Invest," are the initiatives that have a high impact on student results and are also deeply implemented in schools. These are the relatively rare instructional initiatives that enjoy wide support among teachers and administrators and have a demonstrable impact on student results. For example, in some school systems, Data Teams are used by every school every week, and the system-wide impact on student results is significant and sustained (Fullan, 2010; Anderson, 2010). In the upper left-hand quadrant, labeled "Lead," are the initiatives with a high impact on student results but only sporadic implementation in the classroom. For example, informational writing is supported by impressive research but continues to be rarely used, particularly outside of English language arts classes (Kiuhara, Graham, and Hawken, 2009). This is not a problem with the publishers of the writing curriculum, but a leadership issue. We know what to do, but fail to do it. In the lower left-hand quadrant, labeled "Weed," are initiatives that have outlived their usefulness, as they have low impact and are rarely implemented.

In this category we find unused and outdated technology and instructional fads that were announced with enthusiasm but never influenced achievement or professional practice. Finally, the lower right-hand quadrant, labeled "Evaluate," includes instructional initiatives that remain popular but have little or no relationship to gains in achievement. The lack of association with improved achievement does not necessarily mean that an initiative is without value. It is possible that the measurement of impact needs to

BOOK ONE EXHIBIT 1.1

Initiative Matrix

be adjusted. This is the case with some special education initiatives that can significantly improve student performance, but the impact of these initiatives will not be clear if the measurement is grade-level proficiency. An initiative that helps a sixth-grade student improve from a third-grade reading level to a fifth-grade reading level is clearly successful, but at the end of the year, that student will nevertheless be labeled as not proficient at sixth-grade reading. A better measurement of impact would be the extent to which the initiative is associated with more than a one-year gain in student learning. Other initiatives in this quadrant may be in place for political or cultural reasons. Local policymakers and educators may have determined that they are important even though the initiatives are not related to gains in achievement. Intellectually honest evaluation of these initiatives, therefore, requires that leaders are clear that a decision to allocate time and money in that quadrant is based on reasons other than gains in student learning.

Leaders have tough choices ahead of them. The demands of the Common Core will require significant investments of time and money even as those resources are dwindling in many schools. Without additional revenue, leaders must reallocate money and teachers must reallocate time away from other instructional initiatives. Across-the-board cuts only perpetuate the "Law of Initiative Fatigue" (Reeves, 2006) and ensure that teachers will pursue fruitlessly too many initiatives with insufficient time for any of them. Rather, leaders must make tough choices to make 100 percent cuts in some areas and increases in others. A systematic assessment of the impact of initiatives on student achievement is a good way to start that difficult process.

BALANCE: TAKING OTHER IMPORTANT FACTORS INTO ACCOUNT

While the management maxim "what gets measured gets done" may be a truism, the educational corollary—"what is not tested is unimportant"—is unsettling. The nation faces a looming obesity crisis, with an estimated 20 percent of teenagers overweight (Moss, 2011), yet the impact of physical education on student health is rarely monitored in a systematic manner. Accessibility to certain technology resources has a clear impact on student achievement, with a recent study of 997 schools (Davis, 2011) revealing that technology-based interventions for English language learners, struggling readers, and special education students were top predictors of improved test scores, drop-out rate reduction, and course completion, yet the education professionals in technology-related positions, including teachers in libraries, media centers, and technology classes, are often first on the list of budget cuts, because their efforts are not reflected in test scores in an obvious way. While music, drama, visual arts, or extracurricular activities may be the primary source of student engagement for many students, the efforts of these teachers are unlikely to be clearly reflected in assessments of Common Core standards. While we pay lip service to 21st-century skills such as cooperation and communication, assessments of Common Core standards are unlikely to involve teams of students, or to require that they speak or use technology to do more than respond to test questions.

Therefore, educational leaders must establish a clear vision that reflects the values and aspirations of their communities. "Yes," they can say, "we believe that the Common Core offers an important foundation for our students, and we will provide opportunities for every one of them to be successful. However, we are much more than a standards factory. We seek to produce not only proficient students, but people who are curious and engaged. Although our students achieve proficiency in standards on an individual basis, we want them to graduate with experiences that involve the teamwork uniquely provided on athletic fields, in musical ensembles, and in dramatic activities. Our graduates will not only love reading, but also love ideas that they explored far beyond the boundaries of classes devoted to literacy and mathematics." While many educational leaders may express belief in such a statement, the authenticity of that belief will be revealed in how they engage the entire school community in implementing a comprehensive vision that includes the Common Core State Standards, but places those standards into a broader context of challenge and meaning.

SUMMARY

There are five essential questions that educational leaders must explore with teachers, students, community members, administrators, and policymakers as they implement the Common Core State Standards. First, they must consider the moral imperative behind standards, making the case that the Common Core is not just a response to federal requirements or financial incentives, but to the moral imperatives behind standards-based teaching and assessment.

Second, leaders must consider the professional learning needs of faculty and administrators. This process must include some deep reflection on the successes and failures of previous standards and a healthy skepticism about programs that provide mere delivery of standards without deep understanding and application of them at the classroom level.

Third, leaders must dramatically improve the way that they monitor standards implementation. In the past decade, monitoring has largely been limited to periodic testing of students, a process that was seldom linked explicitly to the specific professional practices of teachers and administrators. Knowing that test scores change without understanding the adult actions behind those scores will not provide a framework for sustainable change. Fortunately, there are effective models, such as the Implementation Audit, that allow leaders to examine systematically the link between adult actions and student results.

Fourth, leaders face an era of growing educational demands accompanied by dwindling resources. The most important strategic decision for educational leaders will be allocating time, money, and intellectual energy to support the Common Core and simultaneously deciding which initiatives and programs are not worthy of time, attention, and resources.

Fifth, even as leaders support the CCSS, they must also maintain support for community values that are not assessed in standards-referenced exams. The value of community service, visual and performing arts, fair play, and personal health, to name just a few, cannot be ignored as leaders pursue the Common Core. Indeed, if we have learned anything in the past two decades of standards-based reform, it is that standards are not enough. Educational leaders must help to create a context for learning that includes far more than lists of academic requirements and tables of test scores.

Twenty years ago, Grant Wiggins set a tone that can still guide us today in his important article "Standards, Not Standardization"

(Wiggins, 1991). Today, the implementation of the Common Core standards need not result in the standardization of teaching and learning with the pursuit of proficiency as our highest aim. One of the most empowering and important activities for schools preparing for the CCSS is to create a continuum of learning activities that not only include the requirements of the standards, but also create opportunities for students to far exceed those standards. This is a way to embrace teacher creativity and defeat the notion that the use of educational standards must lead to the stultifying standardization of classrooms.

Finally, school leaders and policymakers should resist the temptation to "wait for Washington" or other educational authorities to start making important preparations for the Common Core. Although some states may not change assessments until 2014, schools that start preparing now will have the greatest success—and the least anxiety—when the Common Core is fully implemented.

References

Ainsworth, L., & Viegut, D. (2006). *Common formative assessments: How to connect standards-based instruction and assessment.* Thousand Oaks, CA: Corwin.

Anderson, K. (2010). *Data teams: Success stories* (vol. 1). Englewood, CO: Lead + Learn Press.

Colvin, G. (2008). *Talent is overrated: What really separates world-class performers from everybody else.* New York: Portfolio.

Darling-Hammond, L. (2010). *The flat world and education: How America's commitment to equity will determine our future.* New York: Teachers College Press.

Davis, M. R. (2011, March 17). Researchers evaluate tech.-oriented, personalized learning. *Education Week, 30*(25), 38.

DuFour, R., & Marzano, R. J. (2009, February). High-leverage strategies for principal leadership. *Educational Leadership, 66*(5), 62–69.

Friedman, T. L. (2005). *The world is flat.* New York: Farrar, Straus and Giroux.

Fullan, M. (2010). *All systems go: The change imperative for whole system reform.* Thousand Oaks, CA: Corwin.

Hattie, J. (2009). *Visible learning: A synthesis of over 800 meta-analyses relating to achievement.* New York: Routledge.

Ingersoll, R., & Perda, D. (2009). *How high is teacher turnover and is it a problem?* Consortium for Policy Research in Education, University of Pennsylvania.

Kiuhara, S. A., Graham, S., & Hawken, L. S. (2009, February). Teaching writing to high school students: A national survey. *Journal of Educational Psychology, 101*(1), 136–160.

Moss, M. (2011, March 27). Philadelphia school battles students' bad eating habits, on campus and off. Retrieved April 5, 2011 from www.nytimes.com/2011/03/28/us/28food.html?pagewanted=1

Peery, A. (2011). *The data teams experience: A guide for effective meetings.* Englewood, CO: Lead + Learn Press.

Pink, D. H. (2009). *Drive: The surprising truth about what motivates us.* New York: Riverhead Books.

Popham, W. J. (2008). *Transformative assessment.* Alexandria, VA: ASCD.

Reeves, D. B. (2002). *The daily disciplines of leadership: How to improve student achievement, staff motivation, and personal organization.* San Francisco: Jossey-Bass.

Reeves, D. B. (2006). *The learning leader: How to focus school improvement for better results.* Alexandria, VA: ASCD.

Reeves, D. B. (2008). *Assessing educational leaders: Evaluating performance for improved individual and organizational results* (2nd ed.). Thousand Oaks, CA: Corwin.

Reeves, D. B. (2010, May 12). Common standards: From what to how: How common core standards should influence teaching. *Education Week, 29*(31), 32–33.

Reeves, D. B. (2011). *Finding your leadership focus: What matters most for student success.* New York: Teachers College Press.

Stiggins, R. J., Arter, J., Chappuis, J., & Chappuis, S. (2004). *Classroom assessment for student learning: Doing it right, using it well.* Portland, OR: Assessment Training Institute.

Wiggins, G. (1991, February). Standards, not standardization: Evoking quality student work. *Educational Leadership, 48*(5), 18–25.

Yatvin, J. (2011, March 30). Linking pay and class size hurts teaching quality (Letter to the editor). *Education Week, 30*(26), 26.

Yazzie-Mintz, E. (2010). *Charting the path from engagement to achievement: A report on the 2009 high school survey of student engagement.* Bloomington, IN: Center for Evaluation & Education Policy.

Gaining a Deeper Understanding of the Common Core State Standards: The Big Picture

Maryann D. Wiggs

The Hope and the Promise

The Common Core State Standards Initiative (CCSSI), coordinated by the National Governors Association Center for Best Practices (NGA Center) and the Council of Chief State School Officers, released the Common Core State Standards for English language arts (ELA) and mathematics in June 2010. Both the English language arts and the mathematics standards have enjoyed widespread support, and have been voluntarily adopted by the majority of states across the country. The Common Core represents a major opportunity to improve the quality of education for our nation's youth. This chapter provides a big-picture overview of some of the design and organizational features of the standards that will be useful when developing an informed, multiyear implementation plan. To access all CCSS documents and available resources, visit www.corestandards.org.

The K–12 Common Core standards incorporate the strengths of and lessons learned from current state standards and then further increase grade-level expectations by benchmarking against the rigorous standards of countries with high-performing school systems. Informed by evidence and research, the CCSS documents define what students should know and be able to do at every level of schooling in ELA and mathematics to ensure that students who graduate from high school are prepared to succeed in college and careers in a shifting global economy and society (CCSSI, 2010a).

It is the hope and the promise of the CCSSI that we come together as a nation to address the disparity in achievement exhibited across the country, and thereby increase equitable access for many more students so that they can transition from high school to college and the workforce prepared to succeed. The development of these focused, specific, and rigorous common academic standards is the cornerstone of an interconnected accountability structure to attain higher levels of learning and improve achievement for all students, not just some students. Indeed, if we are to fully realize this vision, then leaders at all levels must galvanize efforts to translate the standards into actions that are equally focused and explicit in improving the quality of instruction in classrooms across the United States.

Centering Force

Standards are the centering force for schooling. Taken together, standards and assessments are the core of quality instruction. Specific and clearly stated, the Common Core standards are the "*what*" kids should know and be able to do, and assessments are the "*how*" we know that students have achieved proficiency. According to the Thomas B. Fordham Institute, "the Common Core turned out to be a commendable product, a significant improvement in academic expectations and clarity for the vast majority of states" (Finn and Petrilli, 2010, p. 2). How school plays out in terms of grade-level groupings, course design, curriculum maps, report cards, intervention systems, and accountability systems is all grounded on the hope and the promise that we get the standards right in the first place. The Fordham Institute further notes that "standards describe the destination that schools and students are supposed to reach, but by themselves have little power to effect change. Much else needs to happen to successfully journey toward that destination" (Finn and Petrilli, 2010, p. 2). The "much else" that needs to happen is the close alignment of the *written, taught, tested,* and *attained* curriculum.

Transitioning to the Common Core

A map provides its user with a broad perspective of the terrain to be navigated and, when consulted throughout a journey, serves to orient the traveler. Similarly, the general overview provided in this chapter on gaining a deeper understanding of the CCSS provides a broad perspective of the infrastructure and learning progressions within the standards. It is, however, no substitute for actually digging into and conducting a careful reading of the standards documents and accompanying appendices in their entirety. And don't go it alone. The many contributing authors and organizations of the CCSSI created an excellent product by working together; understanding the Common Core and developing an implementation plan will also be best accomplished through collaboration.

Navigating the CCSS terrain is merely the starting point of the arduous journey of implementing the standards within the context of diverse educational settings. Educators will have to share the load and stick together to ensure that all students reach the summit of what is possible for their future. As an educational community, the CCSSI provides a marvelous opportunity to form collaborative partnerships across time zones to leverage the strenuous work of implementing these shared standards. There is power in our collective capacity that we can harness as we build networks to engage in the shared work of designing high-quality, rigorous curriculum units of study, robust performance assessment tasks, and aligned instructional and technological resource materials. There is equal power in reaching mutual decisions to put aside strategies that do not work and/or that contribute to the diffusion of our efforts.

As you solidify your understanding of the Common Core, consider the distance your school or district must travel to achieve our nation's shared goals. The 100-day action plan described in Chapter Six provides a framework for planning, implementing, and monitoring the Common Core. The 100-day action plan CCSS framework will provide an organized perspective regarding the terrain to be navigated when implementing the CCSS and, when consulted throughout the journey, will serve to orient educators on their journey to CCSS implementation.

GETTING FAMILIAR WITH THE CCSS FOR K–12 ENGLISH LANGUAGE ARTS AND LITERACY IN HISTORY/SOCIAL STUDIES, SCIENCE, AND TECHNICAL SUBJECTS

To fully appreciate the design and organization of the K–12 CCSS for English language arts and literacy in history/social studies, science, and technical subjects, it is important to understand the special role of the four sets of strand-specific college and career readiness (CCR) anchor standards. There are a total of 32 CCR anchor standards divided into four literacy strands. The reading strand has ten CCR anchor standards, the writing strand has ten, the speaking and listening strand has six, and the language strand has six. Each set of anchor standards defines broad literacy expectations for college and career readiness. It may be useful to think of each of the four sets of CCR anchor standards as the "North Star" for the literacy strand it represents, providing clear orientation as students advance on the path toward college and career readiness.

As noted in Exhibit 2.1, there is a direct, one-to-one correspondence between each grade-specific standard and a CCR anchor standard. Grade-specific standards define end-of-year expectations in each of the four literacy strands. The standards are based on a mastery model of learning whereby students are expected to demonstrate proficiency in each year's grade-specific standard and further advance knowledge and skills as they progress through the grades (CCSSI, 2010b, p. 8).

Design and Organization

The standards document for K–12 English language arts and literacy in history/social studies, science, and technical subjects is divided into three main sections with three appendices. Exhibit 2.2 illustrates how each section is organized around K–5 literacy content; 6–12 literacy content; and a separate section for 6–12 standards for literacy in history/social studies, science, and technical subjects. The reading strand is further divided into K–5 reading standards for foundational skills, K–12 reading standards

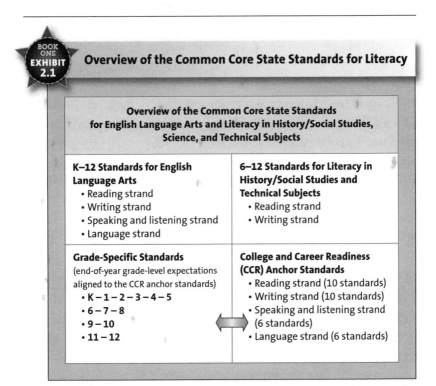

BOOK ONE EXHIBIT 2.1

Overview of the Common Core State Standards for Literacy

Overview of the Common Core State Standards for English Language Arts and Literacy in History/Social Studies, Science, and Technical Subjects

K–12 Standards for English Language Arts	**6–12 Standards for Literacy in History/Social Studies and Technical Subjects**
• Reading strand • Writing strand • Speaking and listening strand • Language strand	• Reading strand • Writing strand
Grade-Specific Standards (end-of-year grade-level expectations aligned to the CCR anchor standards) • K – 1 – 2 – 3 – 4 – 5 • 6 – 7 – 8 • 9 – 10 • 11 – 12	**College and Career Readiness (CCR) Anchor Standards** • Reading strand (10 standards) • Writing strand (10 standards) • Speaking and listening strand (6 standards) • Language strand (6 standards)

for literature, and K–12 reading standards for informational text. The three appendices are critical reading for bringing the standards to life in the classroom. The appendices provide exemplars of student performance tasks and, more importantly, descriptors for understanding the level of rigor and application intended in the grade-specific standards.

Learning Progressions and the Spiral Effect

Among the most salient accomplishments in the design considerations of the ELA standards document are the learning path-

BOOK ONE EXHIBIT 2.2 English Language Arts Standards Organization

Organization of the English Language Arts Standards

Section I: Standards for ELA and Literacy in History/Social Studies, Science, and Technical Subjects K–5

- Reading standards for literature K–5 (RL)
- Reading standards for informational text K–5 (RI)

- Reading standards: foundational skills K–5 (RF)

- Writing standards K–5 (W)

- Speaking and listening standards K–5 (SL)

- Language standards K–5 (L)

Section II: Standards for English Language Arts 6–12

- Reading standards for literature 6–12 (RL)
- Reading standards for informational text 6–12 (RI)

- Writing standards 6–12 (W)

- Speaking and listening standards 6–12 (SL)

- Language standards 6–12 (L)

Section III: Standards for Literacy in History/Social Studies, Science, and Technical Subjects 6–12

- Reading standards for literacy in history/social studies 6–12 (RH)

- Reading standards for literacy in science and technical subjects 6–12 (RST)

- Writing standards for literacy in history/social studies, science, and technical subjects 6–12 (WHST)

Appendix A provides supplementary material on reading exemplars and foundational skills, definitions of writing, the role of speaking and listening, an overview of progressive language skills, a glossary of terms, and a detailed discussion on text complexity. Contains 43 pages.

Appendix B provides numerous sample texts illustrating the complexity, quality, and range of reading appropriate for various grade levels with accompanying sample performance tasks. The standards intentionally do not offer a reading list, as school districts and states must decide on curriculum. Contains 183 pages.

Appendix C provides annotated samples demonstrating at least adequate performance in student writing at various grade levels. Contains 107 pages.

ways that students follow as they advance from one grade-specific standard to the next, leading to proficiency in each CCR anchor standard. While the anchor standards taken together serve to provide focus on what matters most for college and career readiness in the area of English language arts, coherence is accomplished by the explicit articulation of knowledge and skills along the learning progressions. The specificity of the content within the learning progressions makes visible and clear the expectations for student learning (CCSSI, 2010a). In other words, the grade-specific standards clearly define competence at every level of schooling.

The "spiral effect" is a useful metaphor for further understanding how the learning progressions are structured to provide support for many more students to both access and accelerate through the learning pathways.

Consider the following definitions from the Merriam-Webster online dictionary (www.merriam-webster.com):

Spiral when used as an *adjective:*

- Winding around a center or pole and gradually receding from or approaching it.
- Of or relating to advancement to higher levels through a series of cyclical movements.

Spiral when used as a *noun:*

- The path of a point in a plane moving around a central point while continuously receding from or approaching it.
- A continuous spreading and accelerating increase or decrease.

The spiral effect metaphor relates to the ascending level of difficulty embedded in the content of each grade-specific standard as it approaches the CCR anchor standard. The CCR standards serve as the central points or significant learning expectations toward which all grade-specific standards aspire. As students move along the plane of a particular learning trajectory they study the same expectation each year at ever-increasing increments of complexity and sophistication. Gradual cycling through repeated exposure to iterations of the same concepts and processes each year breaks complex learning expectations into manageable teaching and learning targets. Exhibit 2.3 illustrates how concepts and skills for a given standard are both reinforced and expanded as students advance through the grades along the learning progressions.

Overview of the Reading Strand

The reading standards for literature and informational text are composed of nine standards focused on reading comprehension and one standard focused on the range and level of text complexity. The nine reading comprehension standards are further broken down into specific standards around the themes of "key ideas and details," "craft and structure," and "integration of knowledge and ideas." Standard 10 defines a grade-by-grade "staircase" of increasing text complexity that progresses from early reading to the CCR level (CCSSI, 2010b, p. 8).

The standards demand that the quality and the volume of what students read expand in order for students to become proficient at higher levels of thinking and reading comprehension. Guidance is provided regarding the breadth and depth of required reading content that paints a portrait of a literate citizen; content

Spiral Effect for Reading Standard 3

Example of Grade-Specific Standards for Reading Standard 3

The example below illustrates how skills and concepts for end-of-year, grade-specific expectations for a given standard are both reinforced and expanded as students advance through the grades. The result is a *"spiral effect"* where students repeatedly practice mastered competencies from the year prior in the context of new competencies being "added" each year as the standard increases in complexity and sophistication. New skills and concepts added to each grade level from the year prior are noted in **bold**.

R.CCR.3	**CCR Reading Anchor Standard 3:** **Analyze how and why individuals, events, and ideas develop and interact over the course of a text.**	**=**
RL.11-12.3 Grade 11–12 students:	Analyze the **impact of the author's choices regarding how to develop and relate elements** of a story or drama **(e.g., where a story is set, how the action is ordered, how the characters are introduced and developed)**.	**+**
RL.9–10.3 Grade 9–10 students:	Analyze how **complex characters (e.g., those with multiple or conflicting motivations) develop over the course of a text,** interact with other characters, **and advance the plot or develop the theme.**	**+**
RL.8.3 Grade 8 students:	Analyze how particular **lines of dialogue or incidents** in a story or drama **propel the action, reveal aspects of a character, or provide a decision.**	**+**
RL.7.3 Grade 7 students:	**Analyze** how particular **elements** of a story or drama **interact (e.g., how setting shapes the characters or plot).**	**+**
RL.6.3 Grade 6 students:	Describe **how** a particular story's or drama's plot **unfolds in a series of episodes as well as how** the characters **respond or change as the plot moves toward resolution.**	**+**
RL.5.3 Grade 5 students:	**Compare and contrast two or more** characters, settings, or events in a story or drama, drawing on specific details in the text **(e.g., how characters interact).**	**+**
RL.4.3 Grade 4 students:	Describe **in depth** a character, setting, **or event** in a story **or drama,** drawing on specific details in the text (e.g., a character's thoughts, words, or actions).	**+**
RL.3.3 Grade 3 students:	Describe characters in a story **(e.g., their traits, motivations, or feelings) and explain how their actions contribute to the sequence of events.**	**+**
RL.2.3 Grade 2 students:	Describe **how** characters in a story **respond to major events and challenges.**	**+**
RL.1.3 Grade 1 students:	**Describe** characters, settings, and major events in a story, **using key details.**	**+**
RL.K.3 Kindergarten students:	**With prompting and support, identify characters, settings, and major events in a story.**	**+**

Source: Adapted from CCSSI, 2010b, pp. 11, 12, 36, 38.

should include, but not be limited to, classic and contemporary literature, myths and poems, dramas, stories from diverse cultures, U.S. founding documents, and American literature. Three appendices serve as companion documents for the CCSS for English language arts. Appendix A provides a complete discussion about why text complexity matters and explains a three-part model for measuring text complexity. Appendix B, featured in Exhibit 2.4, provides both text exemplars and sample performance tasks to illustrate the complexity, quality, and range of student reading and application at various grade levels. While the titles presented in Appendix B provide useful examples, all decisions regarding selection of high-quality literature and informational texts are left to each individual school and district (CCSSI, 2010c and 2010d).

Throughout the Common Core, tremendous emphasis is placed on students' ability to closely read and interact with increasingly challenging literature and informational text. While the K–5 reading standards represent a balance between literature and informational text, there is a shift when students reach the 6–12 reading standards toward a greater focus on literary nonfiction. Aligned with the National Assessment of Educational Progress (NAEP) Reading Framework, the CCSS ELA standards indicate that by the senior year in high school, 70 percent of the sum of student reading across the grade should be informational text (CCSSI, 2010b, p. 5). At all levels, students are expected to actively engage in making within-text and between-text connections while using analytical thinking skills to synthesize textual evidence (TCRWP, 2010).

Common Core State Standards Appendix B

Text Exemplars and Sample Performance Tasks

Appendix B	Text exemplars are provided as examples *only* to illustrate the complexity, quality, and range of student reading at various grade levels.	Sample performance tasks are provided to further illustrate the application of the standards to texts of sufficient complexity, quality, and range. (Words in italic represent elements from particular standards, which are listed at the end of each task in brackets.)
Grade 11–CCR Text Exemplars	**Stories:** Hawthorne, Nathaniel. *The Scarlet Letter* **Drama:** Hansberry, Lorraine. *A Raisin in the Sun* **Poetry:** Neruda, Pablo. "Ode to My Suit." **Informational Text:** Tan, Amy. "Mother Tongue." Lagemann, Ellen Condliffe. "Education." Gibbs, W. Wayt. *Untangling the Root of Cancer*	**Sample Performance Task:** Students *analyze* the first impressions given of Mr. and Mrs. Bennet in the opening chapter of *Pride and Prejudice* based on *the setting* and how the *characters are introduced.* By comparing these first impressions with their later understanding based on how the *action is ordered* and the *characters develop* over the course of the novel, students understand the *impact* of Jane Austen's *choices* in *relating elements of a story.* [**RL.11–12.3**]
Grades 9–10 Text Exemplars	**Stories:** Steinbeck, John. *The Grapes of Wrath* **Drama:** Shakespeare, William. *The Tragedy of Macbeth* **Poetry:** Poe, Edgar Allan. "The Raven." **Informational Text:** Washington, George. "Farewell Address." Brown, Dee. *Bury My Heart at Wounded Knee* Walker, Jearl. "Amusement Park Physics."	**Sample Performance Task:** Students *analyze how* the *character* of Odysseus—a "man of twists and turns"—reflects *conflicting motivations* through his *interactions with other characters* in the epic poem. They articulate how his conflicting loyalties during this long and complicated journey home from the Trojan War both *advance the plot* of Homer's epic and *develop themes.* [**RL.9–10.3**]
Grades 6–8 Text Exemplars	**Stories:** Taylor, Mildred D. *Roll of Thunder, Hear My Cry* **Drama:** Goodrich, Frances, and Albert Hackett. *The Diary of Anne Frank: A Play* **Poetry:** Whitman, Walt. "O Captain! My Captain!" **Informational Text:** Adams, John. "Letter on Thomas Jefferson." Lord, Walter. *A Night to Remember*	**Sample Performance Task:** Students analyze how the playwright Louise Fletcher uses *particular elements* of drama (e.g., setting and dialogue) to create dramatic tension in the play *Sorry, Wrong Number.* [**RL.7.3**]

BOOK
ONE
**EXHIBIT
2.4**

Common Core State Standards Appendix B *(continued)*

Grades 4–5 Text Exemplars	**Stories:** Farley, Walter. *The Black Stallion* Saint-Exupery, Antoine de. *The Little Prince* **Poetry:** Sandburg, Carl. "Fog." Nichols, Grace. "They Were My People."	**Sample Performance Task:** Students read Natalie Babbitt's *Tuck Everlasting* and *describe in depth* the idyllic *setting* of the story, *drawing on specific details in the text*, from the color of the sky to the sounds of the pond, to describe the scene. **[RL.4.3]**
Grades 2–3 Text Exemplars	**Stories:** MacLachlan, Patricia. *Sara Plain and Tall* **Poetry:** Rossetti, Christina. "Who Has Seen the Wind?" **Read-Aloud Stories:** White, E.B. *Charlotte's Web* **Read-Aloud Poetry:** Eliot, T.S. "The Song of the Jellicles."	**Sample Performance Task:** Students *describe how the character* of Bud in Christopher Paul Curtis' story *Bud, Not Buddy* responds to a *major* event in his life of being placed in a foster home. **[RL.2.3]**
Grades K–1 Text Exemplars	**Stories:** Lobel, Arnold. *Frog and Toad Together* **Poetry:** Wright, Richard. "Laughing Boy." **Read-Aloud Stories:** Bang, Molly. *The Paper Crane* **Read-Aloud Poetry:** Hughes, Langston. "April Rain Song."	**Sample Performance Task:** After listening to L. Frank Baum's *The Wonderful Wizard of Oz*, students describe the characters of Dorothy, Auntie Em, and Uncle Henry, the *setting* of Kansas prairie, and *major events* such as the arrival of the cyclone. **[RL.1.3]**

Source: Adapted from CCSSI, 2010c and 2010d.

Overview of the Reading Standards for Literacy in History/Social Studies, Science, and Technical Subjects

The reading standards for literacy in history/social studies, science, and technical subjects follow the exact same pattern as that of the reading standards for literature and informational text. Thus, the design and organization of the standards support literacy instruction as a shared responsibility within the school, as depicted in Exhibit 2.5. This integrated approach to literacy promotes relevant, real-world application of students' reading skills as they analyze, evaluate, and differentiate primary and secondary sources in history and decipher information from scientific diagrams to effectively communicate information and understanding of key concepts and ideas in science and technical subjects. The reading standards for literacy in history/social studies, science, and technical subjects are designed to seamlessly complement content-area literacy (CCSSI, 2010b, p. 4).

Examine the reading standards in Exhibit 2.5 for literacy in history/social studies and reading for literacy in science and technical subjects for grades 6–12 (CCSSI, 2010b, pp. 61, 62), and note how these standards serve to reinforce literacy as a shared responsibility across content areas.

Overview of the Writing Strand

The first nine writing standards are designed around the three themes of "text types and purposes," "production and distribution of writing," and "research to build and present knowledge." Writing standard 10 addresses the range of writing over short and extended time frames. Appendix A of the CCSS for English language arts defines and brings clarity to the rationale for inclusion of the three types of writing showcased in the writing standards. Appendix C of the ELA standards serves to support the writing standards by providing extensive samples of student writing that convey an understanding of adequate performance levels in writing arguments, informational/explanatory texts, and narratives across various grades. Annotations following each writing piece provide further insight into the intent of the standards with regard to what is considered proficient writing at various grade levels (CCSSI, 2010e).

BOOK ONE EXHIBIT 2.5

Example of Reading Standard 3 for History/Social Studies, Science, and Technical Subjects

Example of Grade-Specific Standards for Reading Standard 3, Reading Standards for Literacy in History/Social Studies 6–12

The examples below illustrates how skills and concepts for end-of-year, grade-specific expectations for a given standard are both reinforced and expanded as students advance through the grades. The result is a *"spiral effect"* where students repeatedly practice mastered competencies from the year prior in the context of new competencies being "added" each year as the standard increases in complexity and sophistication. New skills and concepts added to each grade level from the year prior are noted in **bold.**

R.CCR.3	**CCR Reading Anchor Standard 3:** Analyze how and why individuals; events; and ideas develop and interact over the course of a text.	=
RH.11–12.3 Grade 11–12 students:	Evaluate various explanations for actions or events and determine which explanation best accords with textural evidence, acknowledging where the text leaves matters uncertain.	+
RH.9–10.3 Grade 9–10 students:	Analyze in detail a series of events described in a text; determine whether earlier events caused later ones or simply preceded them.	+
RH.6–8.3 Grade 6–8 students:	Identify key steps in a text's description of a process related to history/social studies (e.g., how a bill becomes law, or how interest rates are raised or lowered).	+

Example of Grade-Specific Standards for Reading Standard 3, Reading Standards for Literacy in Science and Technical Subjects 6–12

R.CCR.3	**CCR Reading Anchor Standard 3:** Analyze how and why individuals; events; and ideas develop and interact over the course of a text.	=
RST.11–12.3 Grade 11–12 students:	Follow precisely a complex multistep procedure when carrying out experiments, taking measurements, or performing technical tasks; **analyze the specific results based on explanations in the text**.	+
RST.9–10.3 Grade 9–10 students:	Follow precisely a **complex** multistep procedure when carrying out experiments, taking measurements, or performing technical tasks, **attending to special cases or exceptions defined in the text**.	+
RST.6–8.3 Grade 6–8 students:	Follow precisely a multistep procedure when carrying out experiments, taking measurements, or performing technical tasks.	+

Source: Adapted from CCSSI, 2010b, pp. 61, 62.

One hallmark of the writing standards is the deliberate shift toward a focus on nonfiction writing as evidenced by the emphasis on arguments and informational/explanatory text types. In the early grades, students begin opinion writing that gradually moves toward demonstrating command of composing arguments based on substantive claims, sound reasoning, and relevant evidence. The writing standards are based on the NAEP Writing Framework, expecting 80 percent of student writing by senior year of high school to be on argument and informational/explanatory text, mirroring what matters most for readiness in meeting the demands of college and real-world application (CCSSI, 2010b, p. 5). Another aspect of nonfiction writing emphasized in the standards is the ability of students to conduct research that results in both short and more substantial formal writing projects. The importance of research blended into the standards as a whole is reflective of the need for students to be able to gather, comprehend, evaluate, synthesize, and report on information and ideas quickly and efficiently to answer questions or solve problems (CCSSI, 2010b, p. 4). It is an expectation that students will incorporate technology and digital media in a manner that best supports communicative intent.

Throughout the literacy standards, tremendous value is placed on growing analytical thinkers and critical consumers and providing tools and structures for students to express their voice orally and in writing. In the following example of a grade 8 writing standard, note the level of cognitive demand and rigor and the potential for integration of the reading, writing, and language standards:

Standard W.8.1: Write arguments to support claims with clear reasons and relevant experiences (CCSSI, 2010b, p. 42).

a. Introduce claim(s), acknowledge and distinguish the claim(s) from alternative or opposing claims, and organize the reasons and evidence logically.

b. Support claim(s) with logical reasoning and relevant evidence, using accurate, credible sources and demonstrating an understanding of the topic or text.

c. Use words, phrases, and clauses to create cohesion and clarify the relationships among claim(s), counterclaims, reasons, and evidence.

d. Establish and maintain a formal style.

e. Provide a concluding statement or section that follows from and supports the argument presented.

Overview of the Writing Standards for Literacy in History/Social Studies, Science, and Technical Subjects

The Common Core documents insist that instruction in reading, writing, speaking, listening, and language be a shared responsibility within the school (CCSSI, 2010b, p. 4). Thus, the design and organization of the ELA standards promote writing across disciplines while increasing application within content-area literacy. The K–5 literacy standards for history/social studies, science, and technical subjects are embedded within the K–5 content strands. Writing standards for these areas in grades 6–12 are aligned with the 10 CCR writing anchor standards and complement both the CCSS for ELA writing and subject-area content (CCSSI, 2010b, p. 33).

Examine writing standard 7 for history/social studies, science, and technical subjects, outlined in Exhibit 2.6. Consider the many opportunities for the ELA educator and content-specific educators to work together in mutually reinforcing ways to advance proficiency in conducting, writing about, or speaking about student research.

BOOK ONE EXHIBIT 2.6

Example of Writing Standard 7 for History/Social Studies, Science, and Technical Subjects

Example of Grade-Specific Standards for Writing Standard 7, Writing Standards for Literacy in History/Social Studies, Science, and Technical Subjects 6–12		
The example below illustrates how skills and concepts for end-of-year, grade-specific expectations for a given standard are both reinforced and expanded as students advance through the grades. The result is a *"spiral effect"* where students repeatedly practice mastered competencies from the year prior in the context of new competencies being "added" each year as the standard increases in complexity and sophistication. New skills and concepts added to each grade level from the year prior are noted in **bold**.		
W.CCR.7	**CCR Writing Anchor Standard 7:** Conduct short as well as more sustained research projects based on focused questions, demonstrating understanding of the subject under investigation.	=
WHST.11–12.7 Grade 11–12 students:	Conduct short as well as more sustained research projects to answer a question (including a self-generated question) or solve a problem; narrow or broaden the inquiry when appropriate; synthesize multiple sources on the subject, demonstrating understanding of the subject under investigation.	+
WHST.9–10.7 Grade 9–10 students:	Conduct short **as well as more sustained** research projects to answer a question (including a self-generated question) **or solve a problem; narrow or broaden the inquiry when appropriate; synthesize multiple sources on the subject, demonstrating understanding of the subject under investigation.**	+
WHST.6–8.7 Grade 6–8 students:	Conduct short research projects to answer a question **(including a self-generated question),** drawing on several sources and generating additional related, focused questions **that allow for multiple avenues of exploration.**	+

Source: Adapted from CCSSI, 2010b, p. 66.

Overview of the Speaking and Listening Strand

The six speaking and listening standards are equally distributed around the two themes of "comprehension and collaboration" and "presentation of knowledge and ideas." Both themes reinforce 21st-century skills in establishing the importance of effective oral communication and collaborative discussion to build understanding and solve problems. Along the speaking and listening learning pathways it is expected that students will have multiple opportunities to grow and expand their expertise in leading and participating in collaborative conversations where increasingly complex information and ideas are shared and negotiated. Specific attention is given in the standards to the ability to present evidence and to effectively participate in discussions, whether in one-on-one, small-group, or whole-class settings. Student proficiency at using media and visual display of information to enhance understanding of presentations is embedded within the speaking and listening standards (CCSSI, 2010b, p. 22).

Compare the criteria for proficiency in collaborative communication in the following grade 8 standard example with your own experience participating in a committee meeting, department meeting, or community forum.

Standard SL.8.1: Engage effectively in a range of collaborative discussions (one-on-one, in groups, and teacher-led) with diverse partners on grade 8 topics, texts, and issues, building on others' ideas and expressing their own clearly (CCSSI, 2010b, p. 49).

   a. Come to discussions prepared, having read or
      researched material under study; explicitly draw on
      that preparation by referring to evidence on the

topic, text, or issue to probe and reflect on ideas under discussion.

b. Follow rules for collegial discussions and decision-making, track progress toward specific goals and deadlines, and define individual roles as needed.

c. Pose questions that connect the ideas of several speakers and respond to others' questions and comments with relevant evidence, observations, and ideas.

d. Acknowledge new information expressed by others, and, when warranted, qualify or justify their own views in light of the evidence presented.

Overview of the Language Strand

While the ELA standards organize the language standards in their own strand, these standards are intended to be embedded across the strands of reading, writing, and speaking and listening. The six language standards are organized around the themes of "conventions of standard English," "knowledge of language," and "vocabulary acquisition and use." Thus, the standards emphasize the importance of using formal English in writing and speaking (CCSSI, 2010b, p. 21).

As evidenced in the grade 8 standard example that follows, students are expected to demonstrate increasing independence in navigating unknown words important to comprehension and expression.

Standard L.8.4: Determine or clarify the meaning of unknown and multiple-meaning words and phrases based on *grade 8 reading and content,* choosing flexibly from a range of strategies (CCSSI, 2010b, p. 53).

    a. Use context (e.g., the overall meaning of a sentence or paragraph; a word's position or function in a sentence) as a clue to the meaning of a word or phrase.

    b. Use common, grade-appropriate Greek and Latin affixes and roots as clues to the meaning of a word (e.g., *precede, recede, secede*).

    c. Consult general and specialized reference materials (e.g., dictionaries, glossaries, thesauruses), both print and digital, to find the pronunciation of a word or determine or clarify its precise meaning or its part of speech.

    d. Verify the preliminary determination of the meaning of a word or phrase (e.g., by checking the inferred meaning in context or in a dictionary).

An Integrated Model of Literacy

Consider the following two statements from the introduction to the CCSS for English language arts:

- The standards insist that instruction in reading, writing, speaking, listening, and language be a shared responsibility within the school. (CCSSI, 2010b, p. 4)

- While the standards delineate specific expectations in reading, writing, speaking, listening, and language, each standard need not be a separate focus for instruction and assessment. Often, several standards can be addressed by a single rich task. (CCSSI, 2010b, p. 5)

As we solidify understanding about the design and organization of the ELA standards, it is clear that repeated exposure to big, important themes is woven throughout grade levels and content areas. Exhibit 2.7 demonstrates a few of the possible ways to integrate multiple literacy standards within one rich science task.

GETTING FAMILIAR WITH THE COMMON CORE STATE STANDARDS FOR MATHEMATICS

Like the Common Core standards for literacy, the CCSS for mathematics maintain the goal of and road map for preparing students for college and career readiness. However, the infrastructure of the CCSS for mathematics (CCSSM) differs from the infrastructure of the CCSS for English language arts. The CCSSM utilize a format that best fulfills the function of communicating intent of the standards while fostering focus and coherence along learning progressions in K–12 mathematics. Throughout the document, the CCSSM place an emphasis on mathematical practices and spotlight equal attention on developing understanding of core concepts and fluency with procedural skills. The CCSSM are written to assume mastery, in any given year, of the preceding year's standards (CCSSI, 2010f, p. 3).

The CCSSM document is organized into three distinct sections outlining the standards for mathematical practices, standards for mathematical content for grades K–8, and standards for mathematical content for high school. A glossary and a few tables toward the end of the document provide further clarification of

BOOK ONE EXHIBIT 2.7

Science Task that Integrates Multiple Literacy Standards

Grade 8 Student Performance Task for Science

Students examine claims of products used in advertising, analyze the language used in such claims, design and conduct scientific experiments to test claims, effectively summarize the evidence from their findings in a lab report, and present results for peer review prior to communicating, in writing, the results of their evidence to the product developer.

[RST.6–8.3] Follow precisely a multistep procedure when carrying out experiments, taking measurements, or performing technical tasks.	**[WHST.6–8.1]** Write arguments focused on discipline-specific content.
[RST.6–8.7] Integrate quantitative or technical information expressed in words in a text with a version of that information expressed visually (e.g., in a flowchart, diagram, model, graph, or table).	**[W.8.2]** Write informative/explanatory texts to examine a topic and convey ideas, concepts, and information through the selection, organization, and analysis of relevant content.
[RST.6–8.8] Distinguish among facts, reasoned judgment based on research findings, and speculation in a text.	**[W.8.7]** Conduct short research projects to answer a question (including a self-generated question), drawing on several sources and generating additional related, focused questions that allow for multiple avenues of exploration.
[SL.8.3] Delineate a speaker's argument and specific claims, evaluating the soundness of the reasoning and relevance and sufficiency of the evidence and identifying when irrelevant evidence is introduced.	**[L.8.6]** Acquire and use accurately grade-specific general academic and domain-specific words and phrases; gather vocabulary knowledge when considering a word or phrase important to comprehension or expression.

Source: CCSSI, 2010b, pp. 42, 44, 49, 53, 64, 82.

terminology. Appendix A provides an extensive overview of units of study incorporating the high school mathematics standards as they are played out in two model pathways for either a traditional or an integrated high school course sequence (CCSSI, 2010g). Exhibit 2.8 presents an overview of the CCSSM.

Design and Organization

One hallmark of the CCSSM is the learning pathways along which a student must travel to be college and career ready, as well as the embedded design feature of continually returning to prior learning at ever-increasing levels of complexity. Exhibit 2.9 illustrates the relationship of the building blocks and learning progressions across the K–12 mathematics domains. The development of the mathematics standards began with research-based learning pro-

BOOK ONE EXHIBIT 2.8 Overview of Common Core State Standards for Mathematics

Overview of the Structure of the Common Core State Standards for Mathematics	
K–8	**High School**
Grade	Conceptual Category
Domain	Domain
Cluster	Cluster
Standards	Standards

Source: CCSSI, 2010f.

Mathematics Learning Progressions

Building Blocks and Learning Progressions across K–12 Mathematics Domains										
K	1	2	3	4	5	6	7	8		HS
Counting and Cardinality										
Number and Operations in Base Ten						Ratios and Proportional Relationships				Number and Quantity
			Number and Operations in Fractions			The Number System				
Operations and Algebraic Thinking						Expressions and Equations				Algebra
							Functions			Functions
Geometry										Geometry
Measurement and Data						Statistics and Probability				Statistics and Probability

gressions detailing what is known today about how students'
mathematical knowledge, skills, and understanding develop over
time (CCSSI, 2010f, p. 4.).

Overview of the Standards for Mathematical Practice

The standards for mathematical practice are described as the
"habits of mind" to be developed by students of mathematics. The
set of eight guiding principles portrays the disposition of a profi-

cient math student persevering with engagement of the standards for mathematical content as they grow in mathematical competence. Therefore, the standards for mathematical practice, outlined in Exhibit 2.10, are expected to be embedded in mathematics instruction throughout grades K–12. Instructional notes in the CCSSM document provide descriptors of mathematically proficient students exhibiting each of the eight mathematical practice standards (CCSSI, 2010f, pp. 6, 7, 8).

"The standards for mathematical content are a balanced combination of procedure and understanding. Expectations that begin with the word 'understand' are often especially good opportunities to connect the practices to the content.... In this respect, those content standards, which set an expectation of understanding, are potential 'points of intersection' between the standards

BOOK ONE EXHIBIT 2.10 **Outline of Standards for Mathematical Practice**

Standards for Mathematical Practice

1. Make sense of problems and persevere in solving them.
2. Reason abstractly and quantitatively.
3. Construct viable arguments and critique the reasoning of others.
4. Model with mathematics.
5. Use appropriate tools strategically.
6. Attend to precision.
7. Look for and make use of structure.
8. Look for and express regularity in repeated reasoning.

Source: CCSSI, 2010f.

for mathematical content and the standards for mathematical practice" (CCSSI, 2010f, p. 8).

Overview of Standards for Mathematical Content (K–8)

The K–8 Common Core State Standards for mathematical content are organized in "domains," "clusters," and "standards" within each grade level. The preamble for each grade level begins with explicit descriptors of critical focal points for how best to use mathematics instructional time throughout the school year. Focus, clarity, and specificity are key features of the standards for mathematical content, and no more than four critical areas of study are emphasized in any given grade level. Following the preamble, an overview page succinctly outlines each domain and cluster for a given grade. Grade-specific standards are then organized within clusters.

Domains are larger groups of related standards. Standards from different domains may sometimes be closely related.

Clusters, within the domains, are groups of related standards. Standards from different clusters may sometimes be closely related, because mathematics is a connected subject.

Standards, within the clusters, define *what students should understand and be able to* do at each grade level (CCSSI, 2010f, p. 5).

In grades K–5, students gain a solid foundation in whole numbers, addition, subtraction, multiplication, division, fractions, and decimals, which, taken together, provide students with a strong foundation for learning and applying more demanding math concepts, procedures, and applications (Achieve, 2010). See Exhibit 2.11.

In grades 6–8, students continue to build upon the strong

Overview of Mathematics Domains for Grades K–5

Overview of Grades K–5 Mathematics Domains					
Grade K	**Grade 1**	**Grade 2**	**Grade 3**	**Grade 4**	**Grade 5**
Counting and Cardinality					
Operations and Algebraic Thinking	Operations and Algebraic Thinking	Operations and Algebraic Thinking	Operations and Algebraic Thinking	Operations and Algebraic Thinking	Operations and Algebraic Thinking
Number and Operations in Base Ten	Number and Operations in Base Ten	Number and Operations in Base Ten	Number and Operations in Base Ten and Fractions	Number and Operations in Base Ten and Fractions	Number and Operations in Base Ten and Fractions
Measurement and Data	Measurement and Data	Measurement and Data	Measurement and Data	Measurement and Data	Measurement and Data
Geometry	Geometry	Geometry	Geometry	Geometry	Geometry

Source: CCSSI, 2010f.

foundation formed in grades K–5 through hands-on learning in geometry, algebra, probability, and statistics. The standards for grades 7 and 8 include significantly more algebra and geometry content. Indeed, an abrupt shift in some of the domains takes place between the elementary and the middle school levels. The standards become more aggressive in establishing a timeline for particular concepts, such as establishing basic algebraic proficiency as a universal objective for all students by eighth grade (Confrey and Krupa, 2010). Exhibit 2.12 provides an overview of domains for grades 6–8.

BOOK ONE EXHIBIT 2.12

Overview of Mathematics Domains for Grades 6–8

Overview of Grades 6–8 Mathematics Domains		
Grade 6	**Grade 7**	**Grade 8**
Ratios and Proportional Relationships	Ratios and Proportional Relationships	Functions
The Number System	The Number System	The Number System
Expressions and Equations	Expressions and Equations	Expressions and Equations
Geometry	Geometry	Geometry
Statistics and Probability	Statistics and Probability	Statistics and Probability

Source: CCSSI, 2010f.

Overview of the Standards for High School Mathematical Content

High school standards for mathematical content are listed in conceptual categories, rather than grade levels or courses, as illustrated in Exhibit 2.13. Conceptual categories, taken together, paint a portrait of what the mathematics students must master in order to be college and career ready. In addition to "Modeling," the conceptual categories are "number and quantity," "algebra," "functions," "geometry," and "statistics and probability." Modeling standards are distributed within the five major categories and are noted in the standards document with a star (*) symbol. Standards noted with a plus (+) symbol within the standards docu-

BOOK
ONE
**EXHIBIT
2.13**

Overview of High School Mathematics Conceptual Categories

Overview of High School Mathematics Conceptual Categories	
Modeling	Number and Quantity
	Algebra
	Functions
	Geometry
	Statistics and Probability

Source: CCSSI, 2010f.

ment are beyond the CCR level, but are necessary for advanced mathematics courses, such as calculus, discrete mathematics, and advanced statistics. Standards with a plus (+) symbol are also found in courses expected for all students (CCSSI, 2010f, p. 57). There are a total of 113 mathematics standards for all high school students to master and approximately 43 advanced mathematics standards designated with a plus (+) symbol for students preparing for careers in science, technology, engineering, or mathematics.

An introduction is provided in the Common Core State Standards for mathematics for each of the five conceptual categories that further defines the intent and level of application expected of students mastering the standards. Using a pattern similar to the organization of the K–8 standards, an overview page follows the introduction for each conceptual category, followed by domains, clusters, and standards.

Conceptual categories are overarching ideas that describe strands of content for grades 9–12.

Domains/clusters are groups of standards that describe coherent aspects of the content category.

Standards define what students should know and be able to do.

The standards for high school mathematics call on students to practice applying mathematical ways of thinking to real-world issues and challenges, and they emphasize mathematical modeling. The standards are extremely clear about what is important in preparing students for college and career readiness. High school mathematics standards require students to develop a depth of understanding and ability to apply mathematics to novel situations, as college students and employees regularly are called upon to do (CCSSI, 2010a).

Decisions regarding mathematics course sequence rest with individual schools and districts. Although it is a critical component of implementing the standards, course sequence is not mandated by the standards. Exhibit 2.14, taken from Appendix A of the CCSS for mathematics, demonstrates how two model pathways arrange the content of the standards, in a traditional course sequence and in an integrated course sequence (Achieve, 2010).

SUMMARY

Summary of Activities for Getting Familiar with the CCSS for K–12 English Language Arts and Literacy in History/Social Studies, Science, and Technical Subjects

1. Compare your current grade-level standards with those of the Common Core. Using two different markers, highlight those

BOOK
ONE
EXHIBIT
2.14

High School Mathematics Course Pathways

Appendix A: High School Mathematics Course Pathways	
Traditional Pathway	**Integrated Pathway**
Algebra II	**Mathematics III**
Geometry	**Mathematics II**
High School Algebra I	**Mathematics I**
Pathway A: Consists of two algebra courses and a geometry course, with some data, probability, and statistics infused throughout each.	**Pathway B:** Typically seen internationally, consists of a sequence of three courses, each of which treats aspects of algebra, geometry and data, probability, and statistics.

Source: CCSSI, 2010g.

standards that will remain the same and those that will change. Note the similarities to and differences from your current expectations for students.

2. Become familiar with the K–12 *vertical articulation* of the grade-specific standards by tracing the new concepts and skills added to each grade level to reveal the learning progressions.

3. Examine all four literacy strands together for a given grade level to provide perspective on how the *horizontal articulation* of the strands promotes an integrated model of literacy.

4. Practice the process of "unwrapping" a standard to provide clarity when planning for instruction and assessment.

5. Provide a forum for discussing why the level of text complexity matters and how to measure it. Begin to identify current resource materials in your school's literature collection that illustrate the complexity, quality, and range of student reading at various grade levels.

6. Examine your current student work samples against the criteria in the Common Core grade-specific standards and reach agreement on exemplars of proficient work. Use the student and text exemplars from the CCSS Appendix B and Appendix C to further illustrate the level of rigor expected.

7. Examine current units of study and determine what it will take to "ramp up" the level of rigor and thinking expected in both standards and assessments.

8. Engage special service providers in preparing to design specific interventions and supports to meet diverse needs for advancing all students along the learning progressions.

9. Nurture collaborative efforts by providing time for cross-discipline educators to become familiar with and develop a plan for leveraging shared standards.

10. Persist with the implementation of successful best practices gleaned from two decades of work in advancing standards-based reform efforts.

Summary of Activities for Getting Familiar with the CCSS for K–12 Mathematics

1. Compare your current grade-level mathematics standards with those of the Common Core. Using two different markers,

highlight those standards that will remain the same and those that will change. Note the similarities to and differences from your current expectations for students.

2. Provide explanations with examples of mathematical language used in the CCSS and examine samples of student work illustrating understanding of key standards at various grade levels.

3. Become familiar with the K–8 mathematical learning trajectories by tracing the new concepts and skills within and across domains to reveal the mathematical building blocks and learning progressions, which exemplify how grade ranges build toward or build from one another.

4. Practice the process of "unwrapping" a standard to provide clarity when planning for instruction and assessment.

5. Provide a forum for discussing and modeling the integration of the standards for mathematical practices with the standards for mathematical content.

6. Examine current student performance task results against the criteria outlined in a given standard. Reach agreement on exemplars of what constitutes various levels of proficiency in assessment tasks. Determine what it will take to "ramp up" the level of rigor and thinking expected in both standards and assessments.

7. Discuss how the content of the CCSS will influence the organization of your secondary mathematics program and/or course design. Consider how the high school model pathways outlined in the CCSS Appendix A can provide guidance and support for this discussion.

8. Identify structures for effective teacher professional development opportunities, including mathematical content knowledge and modeling the use of mathematical practices.

9. Engage special service providers in preparing to design specific interventions and supports to meet diverse needs for advancing all students along the mathematical learning pathways.

10. Persist with the implementation of successful best practices gleaned from two decades of work in advancing standards-based reform efforts.

References

Achieve, Inc. (2010, June). Understanding the Common Core State Standards (PowerPoint presentation). Retrieved from www.achieve.org/achievingcommoncore

Common Core State Standards Initiative (CCSSI). (2010a, June). Common Core State Standards (Webinar; PowerPoint presentation). Retrieved from www.corestandards.org

Common Core State Standards Initiative (CCSSI). (2010b, June). *Common Core State Standards for English language arts & literacy in history/social studies, science, and technical subjects* (PDF document). Retrieved from www.corestandards.org/assets/CCSSI_ELA%20Standards.pdf

Common Core State Standards Initiative (CCSSI). (2010c, June). *Common Core State Standards for English language arts & literacy in history/social studies, science, and technical subjects: Appendix A* (PDF document). Retrieved from www.corestandards.org/assets/Appendix_A.pdf

Common Core State Standards Initiative (CCSSI). (2010d, June). *Common Core State Standards for English language arts & literacy in history/social studies, science, and technical subjects: Appendix B* (PDF document). Retrieved from www.corestandards.org/assets/Appendix_B.pdf

Common Core State Standards Initiative (CCSSI). (2010e, June). *Common Core State Standards for English language arts & literacy in history/social studies, science, and technical subjects: Appendix C* (PDF document). Retrieved from www.corestandards.org/assets/Appendix_C.pdf

Common Core State Standards Initiative (CCSSI). (2010f, June). *Common Core State Standards for mathematics* (PDF document). Retrieved from www.corestandards.org/assets/CCSSI_Math%20Standards.pdf

Common Core State Standards Initiative (CCSSI). (2010g, June). *Common Core State Standards for mathematics: Appendix A* (PDF document). Retrieved from www.corestandards.org/assets/CCSSI_Mathematics_Appendix_A.pdf

Confrey, J., & Krupa, E. (2010). *Curriculum design, development, and implementation in an era of Common Core State Standards.* Arlington, VA: Center for the Study of Mathematics Curriculum.

Finn, C. E., Jr., & Petrilli, M. J. (2010, October). *Now what? Imperatives and options for Common Core implementation and governance* (PDF document). Retrieved from www.edexcellence.net/publications-issues/publications/now-what-imperatives-and.html

Teachers College Reading & Writing Project (TCRWP). (2010, September). Spotlight article: Common Core standards alignment update. Retrieved from http://tc.readingandwritingproject.com/news/2010/09

The Future of Thinking and Communicating: Why the Emergence of Adolescent Citizen Journalists Must Impact Educational Decisions

Thomasina D. Piercy

Natalia intently read from her iPod. When she glanced up, I asked, "Do you enjoy reading your iPod more than a traditional book?" The long flight had evoked a desire in most passengers to read, and I observed with great interest the variety of reading modes. Natalia explained, "In the Ukraine, a book costs $50. Household incomes average $200 monthly." I quickly estimated the comparative cost of a book if it were one-fourth of my monthly income, then envisioned bare bookshelves throughout our home. Natalia continued, "I love the feel of a book. I love how it smells. But, I read online books because they are free." Natalia's comments froze my thoughts. Technology is influencing learning with its *relevancy and speed, but in unpredictable economic times, "free" matters even more. I came away from that flight with a new understanding about the changing landscape of literacy.*

How is *understanding* a responsibility? Comprehending deeply builds a foundation for future knowledge. Communication of knowledge and ideas is improved through understanding.

Under Armour CEO Kevin Plank, a young entrepreneur who graduated from the University of Maryland, describes the significant role understanding plays in his success in a video on the *Washington Post* Web site (2008). He explains that his core consumers are ages 8 to 24 and have grown up online, spending a significant amount of time on the Internet. As a result of Plank understanding who his customers are, not just by age, but by how the world of technology influences how they spend their time, whether on Facebook, YouTube, or the Twittersphere, he determined a vital need was to harness this time. As a result, his enormously successful business continues an upward trend on a global level, despite challenging economic times.

Educators would benefit from Plank's simple lessons: Recognize who your customers are, including understanding and harnessing the influence technology plays in their lives. This lesson is one which adolescents have been attempting to teach educators for years. Just as students are expected to fully learn literacy standards determined to be of core importance by adults, educators need to harness the understanding of technology's influence on adolescents' literacy, including its power to impact their lives.

THE CHANGING LANDSCAPE OF LITERACY

Literacy has always had a changing landscape. Improving communication has been a goal of humans since the dawn of recorded history. More than 30,000 years ago, depictions on the walls of caves and on pottery created by prehistoric humans communicated a way of life. The communication of ideas, dreams, and goals has driven humans to leave a legacy to prepare future generations. This need to communicate drove humans to continuously improve methods for sharing their thoughts. More than 2,000 years ago, Socrates, one of the ultimate communicators of his time, believed oral communication was the most effective form of language. Truth and knowledge were passed from one generation to another through oral traditions. However, the oral tradition resulted in a gap in knowledge. The gap existed between those deemed worthy of having the knowledge and those who were not. As a result, knowledge was controlled in the hands of a few.

With Gutenberg's invention of the printing press more than 500 years ago, printed material was not controlled only by a privileged few, but became more accessible to all. For literacy, this tipping point resulted in transitioning communication from hand-written and orally distributed information into widely distributed printed materials. Thoughts could have a greater dissemination. The printing press motivated more people to communicate their personal beliefs and ideas.

There was another tipping point in the 1980s and 1990s, when computer-distributed electronic communication became commonplace. Today, progress in evolving communication mediums can no longer be measured in years. We are on the cusp of another revolution—an electronic revolution of digital literacies: words, pictures, videos, and unlimited social media connections that "enable the bridging and complementing of traditional print literacies with other media" (O'Brien and Scharber, 2008, p. 67). The endless variety and volume of these digital literacies are at once breathtaking and overwhelming.

Recently, literacy's educational landscape has been enduring a torrential downpour of changes in expectations that are hastening its altered appearance. These changes are stemming from several perspectives. One is ACT's (formerly American College Testing) release concerning the skill that differentiated students who equaled or exceeded the benchmark score in the reading section of the ACT college admissions text from those who did not. Students' ability to read, understand, and respond to questions about complex texts was identified as a key variable of success (CCSSI, 2010b, p. 2; ACT, 2006, p. 16). This variable has contributed to the current gap that exists between graduates' capacity to understand complex texts and the demands of both workplaces and colleges. The following literacy facts also point to the need to focus on the literacy gap:

- Just under one in four (24 percent) of all high school graduates who took the ACT exams met all four of the 2010 college readiness benchmarks for English, reading, mathematics, and science (ACT, 2010, p. 8).

- Test scores on ACT assessments remained essentially the same between 2006 and 2010 despite the fact that 30 percent more high school students were assessed by ACT over this period (ACT, 2010, p. 5).

- U.S. students in grade 4 score among the best in the world. By grade 10, U.S. students score among the lowest in the world (Carnegie Corporation, 2010).

- Unemployment rates for those who did not complete high school rose by almost five percentage points between 2008 and 2009 (Gurria, 2010).

The significant changes in literacy are providing educators with opportunities to embrace new concepts and explore potential. Employing new technologies is not another new dilemma; it is an expectation. More so—a *responsibility*. Not necessarily included on written job descriptions, this expectation that educators will remain current with technology as it unfolds is located in the unwritten and often unspoken areas of employee contracts, where general work ethic resides. Educators who typically go the extra mile do not do so for a bonus check at the end of the week. Their reward is intrinsic. Similarly, although incorporating technology to deliver instruction is an expectation, participating in the Twittersphere, for example, may not be your preference for communication. Yet, simply *understanding* what a tweet is and how a tweet is sent provides educators with access to a deeper understanding of how adolescents and adults communicate. In other words, acquiring current technology skills is beneficial because it increases teachers' understanding of adolescent communication, not because it allows educators to communicate with students via social media. With this understanding comes potential to *harness* influence and motivation for complex learning. The exploration of new technology should be viewed as an opportunity, rather than a dilemma.

QUESTIONING CORE LITERACY EXPECTATIONS

Today's changing times are producing significant shifts in core literacy expectations, initiating questions from deep within belief systems. Why has literacy been receiving increased attention during the 21st century? Why does literacy symbolize freedom, which is no longer only representative of the "American Way," but also of the struggle for human rights in many emerging countries as well? When U. S. Press Secretary Robert Gibbs responded to the social uprising in Egypt by explaining basic individual rights include access to the Internet, what new literacy tipping point was reached (2011)? What drives this global literacy symbolization?

Considering a foundational writing skill is to identify the intended audience, these questions are reaching audiences beyond educators. Why has education's audience expanded? Malcolm Gladwell explained during a presentation at the American Association of School Administrators 2010 conference that educators have worked within the safety of the four walls that the education industry has erected around itself. Gladwell's message provided imagery of these walls consisting of educational research, philosophies, top leader selection coming from inside districts, educational degrees that maintain the fidelity of the educational field, and education being relatively uninfluenced by changes occurring outside the safety of the four educational walls. Today's continuous changes in global literacy are greatly impacting educational decisions. Not only are digital literacies our houseguests, we must invite global change to our literacy table.

Accepting that literacy is being impacted from outside education's four walls requires putting our habits of mind (Costa and Kallick, 2008) into practice, including "questioning and posing problems while listening with understanding and empathy." Since the audience has expanded outside our four educational walls, does literacy have the capacity to prevent a global meltdown? Can the collective literacy of a nation's citizenry become the bulwark and bastion for democracy throughout the world? Is trust in the government more evident in a literate populace? And returning to our educational audience, is it the desire of our citizenry to provide a superb education for each and every student enrolled in public, private, religious, and charter schools across the 50 states and the territories that comprise the United States?

This question is promptly addressed in the introduction to the Common Core State Standards: "They [the English language arts CCSS] reflexively demonstrate the cogent reasoning and use of evidence that is essential to both private deliberation and responsible citizenship in a democratic republic" (CCSSI, 2010a, p. 3). What questions may have gone unnoticed in the shadows of intensity on United States standards designed as a Common Core for all? Current issues that are generating literacy questions for educators include: the influence of social media on literacy, the need for educators to compete for funds, a decline in the number of trained reporters during a time of increased availability of information provided directly and immediately, a decrease of jobs requiring only a high school diploma, the correlation of rising health care needs to low literacy rates, and the fact that students' out-of-school minds may be engaged in more rigorous activities than their in-school minds.

Every aspect of literacy is rapidly changing. Our tendency to retreat behind the safety of education's four walls to write familiar five-year plans is no longer a viable option. Today's realm of literacy includes rapid change and continuous communication.

Contributing to today's core literacy questions, which stem from uncertainty, are the tumultuous changes in communication. One area where this is most evident is the decline of newspapers. This unparalleled decline is leading publishers to pose internal questions similar to those in education: How can our nation's leading newspapers make wrenching decisions during a downward-spiraling economy that will contribute to desired outcomes? Or is it that those outcomes, though *desired*, no longer align with the needs of our lives? When the readership declines, the newsroom shrinks, and the independent daily newspaper ceases publication. The *Baltimore Sun* decided to focus resources on creating a new layout design to increase circulation, but their print circulation numbers are still dropping. It appears that large institutions outside the four walls of education also experience inadequacies when trying to climb over the barriers of old thinking. Newspapers' success began in the early 1800s, the same era in which the concept of public secondary schools was initiated. What can education learn from the newspaper industry to keep from walking the same downward path?

The English language arts CCSS are providing a sea change in thinking. They "lay out a vision of what it means to be a literate person in the 21st century" (CCSSI, 2010a, p. 3). The skills and understandings identified in the Common Core have extensive application inside and outside college and careers. As expressed by David Nagel, "Schools need to take their heads out of the sand, be brave and step forward, and truly help the children entrusted to them" (Nagel, 2011). The CCSS courageously model important, strong steps to best prepare students.

One cause-effect impact of the decline of newspaper circulation is a decrease in the number of reporters in the White House pressroom. A parallel literacy shift has occurred during the past few years, with the U.S. president corresponding "directly" via e-mail with millions of citizens. U.S. citizens questioned the ethics of Thomas Jefferson accessing mass communication through the *National Intelligencer* newspaper in 1800. Two hundred years later, we continue to see the ramifications. Immediate raw information, unfiltered by trained reporters' critical questions that delve for underlying truth, is directly available to all. As a result, the phenomenon of adolescent citizen journalists has emerged.

Students' inherent role as adolescent citizen journalists requires them to have literacy expertise and critical thinking skills at rapidly increasing levels. Is this a desired outcome? Whether we desire it or not, this is the reality of our world. As evidenced during the Egyptian uprising, even a military government cannot achieve a desired outcome when that outcome is not aligned with powerful second-order changes. Although the Egyptian government shut down Internet access across the country for five days, on January 28, 2011, an unprecedented action in the history of the Internet, it was unable to sustain the shutdown. Transformational change must be acknowledged and assimilated. It is when change is not feared, but harnessed and understood, as Plank explained, that the benefits of change can be realized.

The fact that the English language arts CCSS openly state that "the measuring tools for text complexity are at once useful and imperfect" and that they have "limitations and none is completely accurate" (CCSSI, 2010b) models how change is not to be feared, and likewise not a barrier to progress because improved models will follow. Directly confronting the complicated issue of text complexity, rather than avoiding it for another five years, demonstrates the ELA CCSS' level of determination for embracing literacy changes. Circling back to the question in the opening of this chapter—Why is literacy receiving increased attention in the 21st century?—it is vital to understand the impact of tumultuous world events on economic and educational climates.

Of particular interest is the pace of change and its inherent literacy connections, as indicated in the news: AIG repays $6.9 billion to the U.S. Treasury; taxpayers are caught in the middle of a costly Fannie Mae lawsuit; the Security and Exchange Commission is under scrutiny for Ponzi investment fraud. Each of these news stories independently represents an intense magnitude of change, but it is when they are perceived as being connected to the others that profound ramifications can be understood. To begin, we need to *understand* how the above devastating changes in our fundamental organizations happened unforeseen in an age when people have access to an enormous amount of information. How was the public caught napping?

When interviewed for *60 Minutes* on March 1, 2009, Ponzi scheme victims said they thought they were "lucky" to be selected by Bernie Madoff (Kroft and Markopolos, 2009). It is evident they made the intentional choice to *not* ask questions about the 12 percent interest they were somehow earning. Adults chose to *not* use the literacy skills that are being taught as vital skills to students. Harry Markopolos, the financial analyst who was the first to discover the scheme, noted that it only took him five minutes to analyze the performance line and realize it was impossible. Then, he did about four hours of mathematical modeling to confirm his analysis. Literacy is no longer an isolated school subject—the need for literacy in all disciplines surrounds students and adults alike. With the inclusion in the ELA CCSS of disciplinary literacy concepts for reading, students will be able to read like a mathematician, historian, scientist, literary critic, or musician—whatever is required—throughout school and into college and careers (Piercy and Piercy, 2011).

In addition, could it be that the general public had accepted experiencing the news as outsiders, viewing a disconnected reality? Polished and tightly controlled, the news media have provided particular perspectives without giving the viewer access to raw data. As a buffer between actual news events and the readership, the news became a black hole, potentially absorbing citizens' intelligent habits of mind—the same habits upon which literacy resides and is crafted. With declines in traditional literacy occurring concurrently with increases in new literacies, desired outcomes for today's citizenry have never been more urgent. With complexity abounding throughout the world, our students need to be better prepared throughout their 21st-century lives. The ELA CCSS document offers a portrait of the students after having achieved the standards. These students will seek to "understand other perspectives and cultures through reading and listening, and they are able to communicate effectively with people of varied backgrounds." Students will appreciate that people from divergent cultures must learn and work together in classrooms and workplaces (CCSSI, 2010a, p. 7).

THE CONFLUENCE: COMMON CORE STATE STANDARDS AND STUDENTS' FUTURE NEEDS

How is the fact that the public was caught napping during the economic crisis any different than adolescents being required to comprehend information chiefly from textbooks, with minimal direct connections to primary materials? How can instruction harness students' reality? How can teaching literacy actions grounded in critical thinking prevent "black holes" from taking hold? Literacy practices, which promote interaction with knowledge, must be taught to ensure our students will have the capacity to understand and apply the rapidly evolving complexities of literacy. These fundamental literacy actions, including skills, strategies, and processes, are vital for literacy development. Over the years, a plethora of literacy recommendations have evolved to guide teachers in providing instruction for learning to read and reading to learn across the curriculum. However, there are core practices vital for students' literacy development. Literacy actions facilitate increased understanding that adolescents are able to transfer into their lives. Examples include skills that have been proven successful by research, such as creating, exploring, inferring, analyzing, and judging. These skills appear frequently throughout the Common Core State Standards. When literacy actions are taught not in fragmentation, and not only as verbs, but as applied skills within the context of media and life, understanding seeps deeply into adolescents' pores (Piercy and Piercy, 2011, p. 21).

Recent economic problems dramatically rose to crisis stature at a global level, in part because of the void between actual world events and the filtered information provided to the public. How distant can a severe educational crisis be? When the National Assessment of Educational Progress provided data indicating that students had not made progress for decades, and educators did not correct the problem, the federal government took control of education with the No Child Left Behind Act. The potential for a crisis exists once again. To address this problem, we must be prepared to acknowledge the current literacy challenge stemming from the need to teach our adolescents in two "languages"—pre-digital and post-digital. As educators, we do not need additional laws developed by noneducators to resolve the increasing gap between students' 21st-century literacy needs and current educational practices. We recognize we cannot wait another 20 years to address the gap that exists between the status quo and teaching literacy practices essential for living in a transparent, connected world. The only question left is, where are we to begin?

INFRASTRUCTURE AT THE CORE

Reading in the 21st century has become a national symbol of the continued security, independence, and affluence of the United States. Driving this symbolization is our desire to provide a world-class education for *each and every student*. Although this chapter is about literacy change, our desire for each and every student to be successful is the same as is was for the previous era. It is enormously disappointing that reading levels did not significantly progress after billions of dollars, trillions of words, and hundreds of millions of hours of professional development were expended during recent decades on improving pedagogical practice. Reading with deep understanding requires relevant instruction and engagement.

The drive for success for every student can be achieved in the 21st century if it is the desired outcome of all participants, including students and parents. Perspective is provided by considering reading progress as a highway begun during the turn of the past century, when the requirements of the nation demanded that part of its population be capable of following multiple-part directions in order to produce goods and services. At the time, literacy required no more than concrete roadways with stoned shoulders. Traffic was light and the literacy demands placed upon students were less complex. But by the cessation of hostilities in 1945, the country had transformed from an agricultural economy to a manufacturing economy, which included the demand for a better-educated population. Not unlike today's beliefs and desires, changes were caused by the pent-up economic problems, social change, and cultural demands of a population that believed the might and right of America required a better-informed populace. Demands drove our country to begin construction of a highway system that continues into the 21st century. This highway system, much like the educational system, required a higher degree of engineering and materials, tailored to providing a driving surface capable of handling heavier vehicles. Reading instruction over the past 50-plus years has been asked to assume heavier loads of students with differentiated learning abilities, ethnic diversity, and economic inequity. The literacy highway, much like the interstate highway system proposed by President Eisenhower, is beginning to show its age. New systems are required for the transportation of literacy during the 21st century.

Today's literacy highway system includes excellent options for engaging students. For example, electronic reading devices such as the Kindle offer much potential for students, including those at risk in reading. The devices provide access to high-interest, low-readability books, offer fluency support provided by the audio capacity, and include a "coolness" factor, all of which are exceptionally motivational. For example, Christina Franklin, in her role as a high school reading intervention teacher, incorporated the use of a Kindle during reading instruction. A high school student

THE FUTURE OF THINKING AND COMMUNICATING: WHY THE EMERGENCE OF
ADOLESCENT CITIZEN JOURNALISTS MUST IMPACT EDUCATIONAL DECISIONS

73

explained what she told her mom about using the electronic reading device after her mom inquired about her sudden excitement about reading. The adolescent said the following:

- No one can see what you are reading, so you have confidence. I do not feel different anymore.

- I am not a person who likes to read. I thought I was not reading a book.

- It is cool because no one can see what book you are reading or what level you are.

- You change the size and brightness. It helps because you do not feel overwhelmed by having so many words on a page. Now I read *every* word!

- It helps me take my time. I do not feel I have to read as fast as other kids because I am not trying to keep up with them as they are turning the pages.

- I feel like I want to read a lot more interesting books.

- Now, I regret what teachers made me read, because I did not like reading it. I would have read a lot more in the past.

- Today, I am reading *Stargirl* on my Kindle and I understand the story!

All this potential—yet it is not without initial hurdles requiring perseverance that must be overcome in school districts: How can students be prevented from shopping in the Amazon store with its easy "one-click" purchase option? How can a system ensure all material is Children's Internet Protection Act compliant? Such perplexing, forehead-scrunching questions could prevent literacy progress and wonderful opportunities for our students to use hand-held devices to learn. Perseverance, coupled with literacy actions such as exploring the potential of new technologies, will provide engagement bound with relevant instruction.

ESTABLISHING CONNECTIONS FOR HIGH EXPECTATIONS

When questions focus on expectations, literacy connections surface. Today's questions coupled with data have indicated a need to greatly increase student expectations, a key characteristic of the Common Core. Expectations framed in past experiences now must embrace new landscapes. The Common Core has incorporated changes in infrastructure capable of supporting the weight of the new expectations.

How are the CCSS intentionally designed to close graduates' achievement gap?

The CCSS are designed to not only close the current gap between graduates' capacity to read and understand complex text, but also, as a result of the cumulative effect of aligned expectations, to prevent gaps in achievement from occurring. Thus, the research-based CCSS are aligned, backward mapped from college and career readiness expectations, from grade 12 to kindergarten. These tight connections integrated with technology expectations provide such a strong structure that states can readily add standards for pre-kindergarten.

How does the ELA CCSS staircase structure of text complexity (Standard 10) support student growth?

While kindergarten and grade 1 do have expectations for students to listen to complex text, grade-specific text complexity demands begin at grade 2. These are identified in Reading Standard 10, a staircase of increasing text complexity. An example depicting the increase in text complexity is shown in Exhibit 3.1.

Equal emphasis is placed on the complexity of texts students are to read and the skill with which they read, so that students show a steady increase in comprehension and intertextuality, or making connections between texts. In grades K–5, the ELA CCSS balance reading of literature with informational texts. For 6–12, the specific category of informational texts and literary nonfiction demands an unprecedented focus, increasing to 70 percent by grade 12. Expectations for the use of digital resources throughout Standards 1–9, connected with the text complexity expectations in Standard 10, increase rigor for all students.

How do the ELA CCSS braid digital and established literacies together?

In recognition of the need to be ready for life in a technological society, the Common Core recognizes that students need the ability to gather, comprehend, evaluate, synthesize, and report on information, and conduct original research to respond to questions and solve problems. It is expected that students will create a high volume and an extensive range of print and nonprint texts in media forms old and new. Consuming and producing media are integrated into specific standards, rather than being a separate

BOOK
ONE
**EXHIBIT
3.1**

Staircase of Increasing Text Complexity Standard 10

Elementary

GRADE 5: By the end of the year, read and comprehend literature (informational texts) at the high end of the grades 4–5 text complexity band **independently** and proficiently.

GRADE 4: By the end of the year, read and comprehend literature (informational texts) in the **grades 4–5** text complexity band proficiently, with scaffolding as needed at the high end of the range.

GRADE 3: By the end of the year, read and comprehend literature (informational texts) in the high end of the grades 2–3 text complexity band **independently** and proficiently.

GRADE 2: By the end of the year, **read and comprehend literature (informational texts) in the grades 2–3 text complexity band proficiently, with scaffolding as needed at the high end of the range.**

GRADE 1: With prompting and support, read prose and poetry (informational texts) of appropriate complexity for grade 1.

KINDERGARTEN: Actively engage in group reading activities with purpose and understanding.

Grade-level text complexity demands begin at grade 2.

BOOK ONE EXHIBIT 3.1

Staircase of Increasing Text Complexity Standard 10 *(continued)*

Secondary

GRADES 11–CCR (COLLEGE AND CAREER READINESS—GRADE 12): By the end of grade 12, read and comprehend literature (informational texts) **at the high end** of the grade 11–CCR text complexity band **independently** and proficiently.

By the end of grade 11, read and comprehend literature (informational texts) at the **grades 11–CCR** text complexity band proficiently, with scaffolding as needed at the high end of the range.

GRADES 9–10: By the end of grade 10, read and comprehend literature (informational texts) **at the high end** of the grades 9–10 text complexity band **independently** and proficiently.

By the end of grade 9, read and comprehend literature (informational texts) at the **grades 9–10** text complexity band proficiently, with scaffolding as needed at the high end of the range.

GRADE 8: By the end of the year, read and comprehend literature (informational texts) in the grades 6–8 text complexity band **independently** and proficiently.

GRADE 7: By the end of the year, read and comprehend literature (informational texts) in the grades 6–8 text complexity band proficiently, with scaffolding as needed at the high end of the range.

GRADE 6: By the end of the year, read and comprehend literature (informational texts) in the **grades 6–8** text complexity band proficiently, with scaffolding as needed at the high end of the range.

Source: Adapted from CCSSI, 2010a.

expectation (CCSSI, 2010a, p. 4). The ELA CCSS listed in Exhibit 3.2 serve as examples of the integration of digital and established literacies (CCSSI, 2010a).

The bottom line is that students who are unable to comprehend complex texts in both digital and traditional formats are unlikely to be ready for the workforce or college. Students who are not ready for either are less able to contribute to a global economy (ACT, 2006, p. 23). Students unable to access and engage in complex information, and do so quickly, will have their capacity to comprehend, think deeply, and communicate accurately throughout their lives severely challenged.

ADOLESCENT CITIZEN JOURNALISTS

If we consider literacy as organic, it is permitted to evolve, emerge, and transition to fit the environment, adapt to the culture, and migrate between populations. Ask your tween, teen, or twenty-something, or someone in any age group under seventy-five, if they have used or know of the use of text messaging. This form of communication is used to convey feelings, make meaning, and to communicate wants, needs, and desires to another person. It also directly challenges language conventions. The variety of dynamic forms of communication have evolved, emerged, and migrated from one electronic device to another and have found their way into our own 21st-century vocabulary. Organic literacy is expanding 21st-century communication, and extending our understanding of reality.

To harness technology's influence further, ask, "What is an adolescent's reality?" Sometimes it includes virtual reality. Take Second Life as an example. When watching a traditional video, distance exists between the viewer and the screen. Even when the

BOOK
ONE
**EXHIBIT
3.2**

English Language Arts Common Core State Standards Examples of Digital Literacy Integration

- Reading Standards for Literacy in History/Social Studies, **RH.11–12.7:** Integrate and evaluate multiple sources of information presented in diverse formats and media (e.g., visually, quantitatively, as well as in words) in order to address a question or solve a problem (p. 61).

- Reading Standards for Informational Text, **RI.7.7:** Compare and contrast a text to an audio, video, or multimedia version of the text, analyzing each medium's portrayal of the subject (e.g., how the delivery of a speech affects the impact of the words) (p. 39).

- Reading Standards for Informational Text, **RH.8.7:** Evaluate the advantages and disadvantages of using different mediums (e.g., print or digital text, video, multimedia) to present a particular topic or idea (p. 39).

- College and Career Readiness Anchor Standards for Reading.

- Literacy in History/Social Studies, Science, and Technical Subjects, **RHST.CCR.6–12.7:** Integrate and evaluate content presented in diverse formats and media, including visually and qualitatively, as well as in words (p. 60).

- Writing Standards, **W.6–12.8:** Gather relevant information from multiple print and digital sources; assess the credibility of each source; and quote or paraphrase the data and conclusion of others while avoiding plagiarism and providing basic bibliographic information for sources (p. 44).

- Writing Standards, **W.K.6:** With guidance and support from adults, explore a variety of digital tools to produce and publish writing, including in collaboration with peers (p. 19).

viewer is *in* the video, the sense of actual distance between the viewer and the Second Life avatar creates a new realm of possibilities for closing the black hole that absorbs relevance. Students experience learning with no barriers. Learning about pyramids? No problem. The student's avatar travels to Egypt and experiences learning as if it were firsthand. It is much like the experience of reading a great book for a book lover—the learner and the learning are one. There are no gaps. This is not to propose that instruction should be in Second Life—virtual life is not a substitute for living. Once again, it is important for teachers to understand and harness the influence that learning has on students when it exists without gaps. As educators continue to increase their literacy capacity, connections between students' in-school learning and their lives outside of school will increase.

Unlike the past, today's citizen journalists include adolescents. Although it is occurring in front of our eyes, the emergence of adolescents as citizen journalists has remained largely unnoticed, or deliberately ignored. One adolescent explained that school rules limiting students' access to the Internet only result in forcing kids to use their cell phones in the bathroom. Rather than banning this technology outright, educators should harness its potential for fostering increased learning and motivation.

Thinking and communicating like a citizen journalist is the ability to communicate the daily events of one's life, from the context in which they are happening, to the world in which people live or work. Citizen journalists do *not* have professional training as journalists. They use technology to immediately communicate with global audiences when responding to and reporting news and information, providing learning in context. As citizen journalists, adolescents are at the right place at the right time to capture events as they unfold on personal electronic communication devices. They use digital literacies, defined as "socially situated practices supported by skills, strategies, and stances that enable the representation and understanding of ideas using a range of modalities enabled by digital tools" (O'Brien and Scharber, 2008). They report unfolding events through their personal perspective. To accommodate citizen journalism around the globe for the mobile Internet age, CNN, as an example, has a free app for submitting news from cell phones (www.cnn.com/mobile/iphone/). The company overtly states that the content "is not edited or fact-checked." Just as much as adults, adolescents now have enormous opportunities to make an impact rapidly around the globe. Educators are absorbing the weight of ACT's results indicating a need for increased text complexity to close the literacy gap, and the Common Core is establishing increased expectations. But could this concept become a dilemma that educators simply skirt around by rationalizing that it is not an educational problem, but one outside of education's four walls? *Responsibility* is what this dilemma amounts to. Resolving cyberbullying, which has had impossible-to-ignore outcomes as drastic as suicide, is an expectation educators are embracing. Adolescents have taken on the role of citizen journalists, whether we like it or not. What can educators do to prepare them for the inherent responsibility this entails?

It is vital for us to *understand* this relevant connection between adolescent citizen journalists and literacy. There are levels of support students can be provided with. As a first step, Will Richardson (2011, p. 25) recommends that educators become "Googleable" themselves by starting a blog or Twitter account, modeling connections, sharing student work online, and practicing reputation management.

Another good practice is expanding students' technology skills, such as flexibly drawing from at least four sources, making forward inferences, and self-regulating the relevancy and efficiency of one's Internet path (Coiro and Dobler, 2007). As the authors suggest, online reading may require active self-regulated readers. These readers would be able to acquire information from multiple sources while applying reading strategies and making forward inferences across a range of multidimensional Internet sites. Although these skills draw upon current ones used with traditional texts, they require a higher level of complex understanding—*supercell complexity.* Just as a supercell results when two tornadoes connect, combining the Common Core's expectations for text complexity with aligned complex student tasks increases expectations for students and educators. Although the expectations are not unrealistic, support is needed.

An additional level of support is awareness that the comprehension skills required for success are also the ones that challenge adolescents who are weak readers. The potential exists, therefore, for technology to increase the reading gap between high- and low-performing students. The need to increase educators' understanding about the difference in cognitive demand between traditional comprehension strategies and online comprehension strategies is increasingly important. To establish clarity, four characteristics of emerging literacies that can guide educational direction include: new social practices, skills, strategies, and dispositions are required for new technologies; education is needed to provide understanding of civic, economic, and personal participation in the world community; new literacies will be newer tomorrow due to rapid change; and emerging literacies benefit from analysis that provides multiple perspectives (Coiro, et al., 2008, pp. 41–42).

Adolescents need guidance in their decisions as they function as sources and recipients of literacy, providing informative connections in a social media environment and today's 21st-century culture. *The Huffington Post* has provided citizen journalist guidelines that apply directly to adolescent decisions. They are shown in Exhibit 3.3.

As a fundamental baseline, the *Huffington Post* guidelines provide a code of ethics for adolescents to apply to their citizen journalist role. These guidelines support students in incorporating publishing standards.

The adolescent citizen journalist components provided in Exhibit 3.4 (Piercy and Piercy, 2011) expand the guidelines while supporting students in applying literacy actions. Three questions guide adolescent journalist thinking:

1. What questions do I need to ask myself to determine the *context* of the source of information?

2. What questions do I need to ask myself when reading *unfiltered* information?

3. What questions do I need to ask *about* myself before preparing information for distribution?

The specific questions on the citizen journalist filter create an adolescent citizen journalist path for applying literacy actions and habits of mind when reacting to information.

Immediate access to primary documents is having a profound impact on human life, government, and economic stability, and news footage is leading to global uncertainty. Instability is increasing as citizens are communicating their demand for better lives. Transitioning from a world of polished, substantiated news to partaking of and being informed by citizens' free news reports requires high-level literacy skills.

Citizen Journalist Standards for Adolescents

Just the Facts	Stick to what you directly observe when reporting a story; Never invent details or embellish facts.
Avoid Hearsay	Follow up and check the facts; Never report something you cannot substantiate.
Omit Irrelevant Opinion	Do not take an opinion when reporting; Sympathize privately, report factually.
Plagiarism and Giving Credit	Always attribute material used from other sources; Quote sources when applicable and with permission.
Fact-Check Your Sources	Check out your sources; Verify any and all information used in the article.
Spelling and Grammar	Check for spelling and grammar; Spell names correctly.
Integrity of Photographs	Never alter or edit; Give credit for the source if not your personal pictures.
Always Identify Yourself	Do not misrepresent yourself when talking with a source; Tell them you are quoting.
Identifying Sources	Use source names if at all possible; Use quotes with their permission.

Source: Palevsky, 2009.

BOOK
ONE
EXHIBIT
3.4

Thinking and Communicating Like a Citizen Journalist

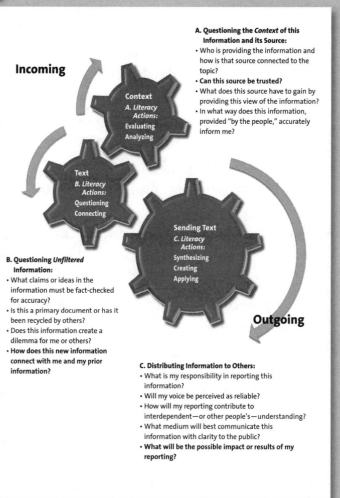

A. Questioning the *Context* of this Information and its Source:
- Who is providing the information and how is that source connected to the topic?
- **Can this source be trusted?**
- What does this source have to gain by providing this view of the information?
- In what way does this information, provided "by the people," accurately inform me?

Incoming

Context
A. Literacy Actions:
Evaluating
Analyzing

Text
B. Literacy Actions:
Questioning
Connecting

Sending Text
C. Literacy Actions:
Synthesizing
Creating
Applying

Outgoing

B. Questioning *Unfiltered* Information:
- What claims or ideas in the information must be fact-checked for accuracy?
- Is this a primary document or has it been recycled by others?
- Does this information create a dilemma for me or others?
- **How does this new information connect with me and my prior information?**

C. Distributing Information to Others:
- What is my responsibility in reporting this information?
- Will my voice be perceived as reliable?
- How will my reporting contribute to interdependent—or other people's—understanding?
- What medium will best communicate this information with clarity to the public?
- **What will be the possible impact or results of my reporting?**

SUMMARY

The definition of literacy is changing as adolescents and adults embrace new technologies. The ELA CCSS support the needed changes in literacy expectations to close the achievement gap of our graduates. Examples of the ELA CCSS' contributions include:

1. Providing a vision of what it means to be a literate person in the 21st century.

2. Identifying specific skills and understandings needed outside of school for college and career readiness.

3. Confronting difficult issues honestly, such as increasing expectations for rigor through raising levels of text complexity for grades 2–12.

4. Establishing foundations for disciplinary literacy instruction to prepare students in grades 4–12 and into college/career to read and understand complex texts.

5. Increasing connections throughout grade-level expectations for students.

6. Providing specific standards aligned from elementary grades through college and careers that include provisions for frequent assessments and monitoring of student growth.

Through understanding and harnessing the influence technology has in the lives of adolescents, educators will be able to achieve the evasive desired outcome of literacy success for every student.

References

ACT. (2006). *Reading between the lines: What the ACT reveals about college readiness in reading.* Retrieved May 29, 2011, from www.act.org/research/policymakers/reports/reading.html

ACT. (2010). *The condition of college & career readiness 2010.* Retrieved May 31, 2011, from www.act.org/research/policymakers/cccr10/index.html

Carnegie Corporation of New York. (2010). *Time to act: An agenda for advancing adolescent literacy for college and career success.* Retrieved June 16, 2011, from carnegie.org/fileadmin/Media/Publications/PDF/tta_Main.pdf

Coiro, J., & Dobler, E. (2007). Exploring the online reading comprehension strategies used by sixth-grade skilled readers to search for and locate information on the Internet. *Reading Research Quarterly, 42*(2), 214–257.

Coiro, J., Knobel, M., Lankshear, C., & Leu, D. (eds). (2008). *The handbook of research on new literacies.* Mahwah, NJ: Erlbaum.

Common Core State Standards Initiative (CCSSI). (2010a, June). *Common Core State Standards for English language arts & literacy in history/social studies, science, and technical subjects* (PDF document). Retrieved from www.corestandards.org/assets/CCSSI_ELA%20Standards.pdf

Common Core State Standards Initiative (CCSSI). (2010b, June). *Common Core State Standards for English language arts & literacy in history/social studies, science, and technical subjects: Appendix A* (PDF document). Retrieved from www.corestandards.org/assets/Appendix_A.pdf

Costa, A., & Kallick, B. (2008). *Learning and leading with habits of mind: 16 essential characteristics for success.* Alexandria, VA: ASCD. pp. 59–68.

Gibbs, R. (2011, Jan. 28). White House press briefing. Washington, D.C.

Gladwell, M. (2010, Feb. 10). Keynote address at American Association of School Administrators conference, Phoenix, AZ.

Graham, S., & Hebert, M. (2010). *Writing to read: Evidence for how writing can improve reading.* New York: Alliance for Excellent Education.

Gurria, A. (2010). Investing in the future. Retrieved June 16, 2011, from www.oecd.org/document/42/0,3746,en_21571361_44315115 _45942378_1_1_1_1,00.html

Kroft, S. (interviewer) and Markopolos, H. (interviewee). (2009, June 10). The man who figured out Madoff's scheme tells *60 Minutes* many suspected Madoff fraud; Says SEC is incapable of finding fraud. *60 Minutes.* Retrieved May 31, 2011, from www.cbsnews.com/ stories/2009/02/27/60minutes/main4833667.shtml

Nagel, D. (2011). Will smart phones eliminate the digital divide? *The Journal.* Retrieved June 16, 2011, from www.thejournal.com/ articles/2011/02/01/will-smart-phones-eliminate-the-digital -divide.aspx

O'Brien, D., & Scharber, C. (2008, September). Digital literacies go to school: Potholes and possibilities. *Journal of Adolescent and Adult Literacy, 52*(1), 66–68.

Palevsky, M. (2009, April 17). Citizen journalism publishing standards. *Huffington Post.* Retrieved May 31, 2011, from www.huffingtonpost .com/2009/04/14/citizen-journalism-publis_n_186963.html

Piercy, T., & Piercy, W. (2011). *Disciplinary literacy: Redefining deep understanding and leadership for 21st-century demands.* Englewood, CO: Lead + Learn Press.

Richardson, W. (2011). Publishers, participants all. *Educational Leadership, 68*(5), 22–26.

Washington Post, The. (2008). *A Conversation with Kevin Plank.* Retrieved June 16, 2011, from www.washingtonpost.com/ wp-dyn/content/video/2008/07/07/VI2008070700969.html

Meeting the Challenge of Rigorous Expectations in the Common Core

Cathy J. Lassiter

We all know Hans Christian Andersen's story about the *Emperor's New Clothes*. The emperor's tailors tell him his new suit is made of a cloth that is invisible to those who are unworthy of their positions. The emperor cannot see the clothes, but is afraid to admit it, and ends up strutting through town proudly displaying the new "outfit," which his loyal subjects (who also do not want to appear unworthy) have convinced him is the finest ever made. However, when a small boy points out that the emperor is actually naked, he comes to understand that he has been sold a bill of goods, hoodwinked, fooled into believing he has something he actually does not. Sadly, this has been the case for many of our high school students over the past decade.

Students and their families, and to some extent teachers, have been convinced by politicians and educators alike that their state standards of learning are rigorous and provide all students with a strong academic foundation for college and careers. Often, state test scores are used to demonstrate how well the state is doing in educating its children. But then reality hits for the students lucky enough to muster SAT scores high enough to be accepted into college. They believe they are ready for the rigors of higher education, only to find they cannot manage the workload, comprehend the complex reading, write at proficient levels, or intelligently engage in discussions requiring higher levels of analysis, evaluation, or problem solving. Have our nation's high school students been sold a bill of goods, like the emperor in the story? The current literature and research on student achievement and state standards suggest that they have.

As far back as 1983, with the release of *A Nation at Risk* (NCEE), concerns about American competitiveness and dumbing down of curriculum have been expressed. Since then, however, the world has become a much smaller place, and megacountries such as China and India have become serious players in the global economy. They want the kind of lifestyle and financial opportunities seen in the West, and they are willing to invest heavily in the education of their children to rocket ahead in the marketplace. The edge previously enjoyed by the United States is shrinking. Leaders in business, government, and education are calling for more rigorous academic programs for all students. They insist on a level of rigor that will prepare and enable the United States to hold its edge, and compete with the emerging economies of the East. The call is for students to be taught 21st-century skills to prepare for a 21st-century marketplace.

Tony Wagner, codirector of the Change Leadership Group at Harvard University and author of *The Global Achievement Gap* (2008a), outlines seven essential skills that his studies reveal we need, but do not currently teach. These skills include critical thinking and problem solving, collaboration and leadership, agility and adaptability, effective oral and written communication skills, accessing and analyzing information, initiative and entrepreneurialism, and curiosity and imagination. Wagner reports that in his many observations of classrooms in the best schools and of advanced classes, fewer than one in 20 engage in instruction designed to teach students to think instead of merely drilling for the test.

Wagner is not alone in advocating such skills. The Partnership for 21st Century Skills has a similar list, and writers such as Daniel Pink, author of *A Whole New Mind*, and Tom Friedman, author of *The World is Flat*, also suggest that thinking and communicating are the cornerstone skills as we move into an ever-changing, evolving economy.

These skills are quite different from the traditional education Alfie Kohn, author of *The Schools Our Children Deserve* (1999), says is typical in American classrooms. The traditional practices and beliefs that dominate our classrooms include: the basics must be emphasized, thinking comes later, facts must be memorized, skills require drills, getting right answers is key, and teaching should be done in small bits and pieces. In a National Institutes of Health study conducted by scholars at the University of Virginia, the key findings support the assertions made by Kohn. After observing more than 2,500 first-, third-, and fifth-grade classes in more than 1,000 mostly middle-class schools spread across 400 public school districts, their findings include (Wagner, 2008a):

- Fifth graders spend 90 percent of their time in their seats listening to the teacher or working alone. They work in groups with their peers only about 7 percent of the time. The same was true for third graders.

- More than 60 percent of a fifth grader's time was spent on improving basic literacy or math skills, which averaged to five times more than the time spent problem solving or reasoning. This ratio was much worse in first and third grades, where 10 times more time was spent on basic literacy than on problem solving.

Wagner contends that the nation is far more seriously at risk today than it was in 1983, when *A Nation at Risk* was published. He asserts that the well-intentioned No Child Left Behind (NCLB) legislation has put all of our children further behind in acquiring new survival skills for learning, work, and citizenship.

The Thomas B. Fordham Institute, an organization that has been studying state standards since 1997, released a comparative study of individual states' standards and the Common Core State Standards in July 2010. The institute's researchers measured the strengths and weaknesses of standards based on clarity, specificity, content, rigor, and general organization. They found that 37 states had standards that were "clearly inferior" to the CCSS for English language arts, and 39 states had standards clearly inferior to the CCSS for mathematics. In 33 states, both the ELA and math standards were deemed inferior to the Common Core (Carmichael, et al., 2010).

This gap in rigor from state to state, and as compared to the CCSS, is supported by data that compare United States students to students internationally on a variety of assessments. As pointed out so vividly in the movie *Waiting for Superman* (Guggenheim, 2010), among 30 developed countries, the United States is ranked 25th in math and 21st in science. When the comparison is restricted to students in the top 5 percent, the United States ranks last. In 1970, the United States produced 30 percent of the world's college graduates; today, however, it produces only 15 percent. Since 1971, education spending has more than doubled, from

$4,300 per student to more than $9,000 per student. Yet, in the same period, reading and math scores have remained flat, and they have risen in every other developed country (Weber, 2010). These alarming statistics bear out in studies with high school students themselves. In the annual High School Survey of Student Engagement conducted by Indiana University, involving more than 275,000 students in 27 states since 2006, only one of two students graduate on time in the nation's urban schools, and one in four fail to graduate on time nationally. More than 60 percent of the students surveyed reported they are not challenged at school, and one of the top three reasons cited for dropouts is the lack of relevance of the work they do at school (Yazzie-Mintz, 2010). This is due in part to the outdated tracking system used by many American high schools, which is based on the old economy. But by 2020, 123 million American jobs will be in high-skill, high-pay occupations, from computer programming to bioengineering, and only 50 million Americans will be qualified to fill them (Weber, 2010).

These data suggest that the United States is at a critical crossroads and the American education system sits prominently at its center. President Obama issued a call to action when he pronounced that whoever "out-educates us today, is going to out-compete us tomorrow." Thus, the nation is engaged in school reform like none before. The creation of the CCSS and their adoption by almost all states as of June 2011 indicate a shift in thinking about national standards designed to prepare all students for college and careers. These common standards offer hope that all U.S. students will have the opportunity to learn in a rigorous academic environment that will draw them in, enable them to compete in the global economy, and keep them engaged in lifelong learning.

RIGOR AND THE CCSS

It is clear that the creators of the Common Core have taken great care to address concerns about rigor in the documents' overall philosophy, goals for the future, design and structure, and emphasis on all students. The CCSS are internationally benchmarked to bring U.S. students up to the academic levels of their peers around the globe. Each standard was selected only when the best available evidence indicated that its mastery was essential for college and career readiness in a 21st-century globally competitive society (CCSSI, 2010, p. 3). The Common Core insists that literacy be a shared responsibility among an entire school, and the inclusion of standards for not only reading, writing, and mathematics, but also for speaking, listening, and using language demonstrates a commitment to improving the literacy of all students.

In its analysis of the rigor of the ELA Common Core standards, the Fordham Institute noted the inclusion of "exemplar" texts for grade spans from kindergarten through grade 12. The institute lauds the standards for specifically including works from authors such as Voltaire, Kafka, and Sophocles for grades 9–10, and Hawthorne, Poe, and Melville for grades 11–12. These lists are accompanied by sample performance tasks designed to specifically illustrate the application of the standards to texts of sufficient complexity, quality, and range (Carmichael, et al., 2010, p. 10).

In writing, the standards are seen as somewhat repetitive, but include much essential content, including the language standards for grammar, usage, and mechanics throughout. The rigor of the writing standards becomes evident in the appendix of student work samples that help teachers understand the kind of writing that is expected across all grade levels and in the three domains of arguments, informative/explanatory texts, and narratives (Carmichael, et al., 2010, p. 26). The Fordham Institute analysis did find flaws in the CCSS, which include: the exclusion of specific text types, genres, and subgenres in the reading standards; issues with scaffolding from grades 3 to 5; and having too many of the writing standards begin with the phrase "with guidance and support from adults," which makes it difficult for teachers to determine exactly what students should be able to do on their own. They still conclude that the ELA Common Core standards are far superior to those now in place in most states, districts, and classrooms. They are ambitious and challenging for students and educators alike (Carmichael, et al., 2010, p. 27).

In the math Common Core, the development of arithmetic in elementary school is a primary focus of the standards. Fractions are developed rigorously, and place value is developed quite well. There are eight standards for mathematical practice that are consistent in grades K–12:

1. Make sense of problems and persevere in solving them.

2. Reason abstractly and quantitatively.

3. Construct viable arguments and critique the reasoning of others.

4. Model with mathematics.

5. Use appropriate tools strategically.

6. Attend to precision.

7. Look for and make use of structures.

8. Look for and express regularity in repeated reasoning.

These eight standards of practice are combined with standards for content that endeavor to balance procedure and understanding.

The Fordham analysis concluded that the math Common Core standards set excellent priorities that are expressed both explicitly and implicitly. In the elementary grades, explicit guidance is provided by identifying the three or four main areas that students are expected to master. The standards also make it crystal clear that arithmetic is the most important topic in the early grades. The CCSS require that students learn math facts that are foundational to their success in higher levels. Fluency, rather than memorization of number facts, is expected for addition and multiplication, as students move into instruction focused on subtraction and division. The standards also discourage the use of calculators in the elementary grades (Carmichael, et al., 2010). Word problems are introduced early and throughout, and multistep problems are included. In middle school, work with fractions and decimals is well utilized in the coverage of proportions, percents, rates, and ratios, which are highly rigorous. High school geometry is also lauded for good coverage of content, and for proofs that are included throughout the standards. Although a few concerns are noted about the organization of the high school content and the omission of explicit foundations for geometry, the rigor of the math Common Core is graded high by the Fordham Institute.

What the standards do not do, however, is mandate particular teaching strategies, writing processes, or metacognitive strategies that teachers should use to get all students to mastery by the end of the year. This will fall on districts and schools. The Common Core is not a curriculum. The standards represent student outcomes by the end of the year in each grade and by graduation.

The curricular building blocks towards mastery of the anchor and grade-level standards are up to states, districts, and schools to determine. The Common Core must be accompanied by a properly aligned, content-rich curriculum to provide teachers with a sturdy instructional framework from which to work (Carmichael, et al., 2010). In his book *Rigorous Curriculum Design* (2010), Larry Ainsworth defines a rigorous curriculum:

> A rigorous curriculum is an inclusive set of intentionally aligned components—clear learning outcomes with matching assessments, engaging learning experiences, and instructional strategies—organized into sequenced units of study that serve as both the detailed road map and the high-quality delivery system for ensuring that all students achieve the desired end: the attainment of their designated grade- or course-specific standards within a particular content area. (p. 8)

Professional development, teamwork, and opportunities for deliberate practice and feedback will be essential for classroom teachers to adjust their teaching to meet the higher expectations in a rigorous curriculum for all students.

TEACHING TO HIGHER LEVELS OF RIGOR

Teaching for success in the Common Core will require a paradigm shift in most schools across the country. Over the past decade, the purpose of school in most districts has become passing the state tests in order to meet NCLB requirements and avoid public embarrassment for poor performance. I have conducted observations in hundreds, maybe thousands, of classrooms at all levels and in states across the nation, and I agree with Tony Wagner's assertion that most children spend their school days preparing in some way for multiple-choice tests. Teachers use flash cards and rapid-fire questioning to drill their students, students quiz each other in hallways, even cafeteria workers quiz children as they come through the lunch line. The focus is on rote memorization of facts, correct answers, and quick responses. Very rarely do we find schools with the vision of teaching for critical thinking and communicating. Very rarely is the learning from one year strongly connected to the previous and next years. Very rarely do we see students engaged in debates and discussion where their opinion, based on evidence, is the focus. And very rarely, if ever, do we see lessons designed to improve students' speaking and listening skills. But this is precisely what is expected in the Common Core.

Before we can discuss specific teaching strategies, we must take stock of where we are in our collective beliefs about the Common Core State Standards and our outlook about what is possible for all students. Therefore, I am suggesting a two-pronged approach to CCSS implementation, along with specific teaching practices that are essential to transitioning our classrooms from memorization and regurgitation rooms to rigorous learning labs.

MEMORIZATION TO RIGOROUS LEARNING: THE FIRST PRONG

The first prong deals outwardly with the beliefs of students, teachers, and principals about students' capacity to master the Common Core, and the school's capacity to get them there. Do we believe all students can master the new skills and content? What is our mindset about teaching all students the Common Core? Do staff members have a fixed mindset or a growth mindset? Those with a fixed mindset believe that intelligence is static (Dweck, 2006). One is either smart or not. Some people are just naturally smart and talented, and conversely, some are not. Those with a fixed mindset believe that what the teacher does matters very little—that the teacher has low efficacy. People with a growth mindset believe that intelligence can be developed with the right support and instruction. Teachers with a growth mindset help students see the value of hard work and effort. They believe anyone can learn anything with persistence and effort.

There are multiple studies that support the power of a growth mindset, many of them conducted by Carol Dweck, researcher and professor of psychology at Stanford University. Dweck has conducted studies with hundreds of students. In her studies, when children are taught a growth mindset and learn that the brain is a muscle that should be exercised to get stronger, students persist through challenges that they would typically give up on. They understand their struggle and hard work is making their brain stronger. When students are told by their teachers that they are naturally smart and learning comes easily, they attempt to hide any difficulties or struggles they have with learning. Those students have come to believe that if they have to struggle, they must not be smart anymore (Dweck, 2006). Dweck maintains that students who have a fixed mindset can still develop a growth mindset, with instruction and support, and that teachers who have a fixed mindset can develop a growth mindset that allows them to believe in all students, with information and teamwork.

Dweck's notion of mindset is also supported in the literature. In 2000, Arthur Costa and Bena Kallick, authors of the *Habits of Mind* books, wrote, "When people think of their intelligence as something that grows incrementally, they are more likely to invest the energy to learn something new or to increase their understanding and mastery of tasks" (p. 3). Also supporting this approach are Lauren Resnick and Megan Williams Hall, who wrote:

> Children develop cognitive strategies and effort-based beliefs about their intelligence—the habits of mind associated with higher order learning—when they are continually pressed to raise questions, accept challenges, find solutions that are not immediately apparent, explain concepts, justify their reasoning and seek information. When we hold children accountable for this kind of intelligent behavior, they take it as a signal that we think they are smart, and they come to accept this judgment. The paradox is that children become smart by being treated as if they already are intelligent. (Resnick and Hall, 1998)

At the end of Benjamin Bloom's career he said that after 40 years of traveling all over the world, he concluded that just about any person can learn anything, given quality instruction and support along the way. He only excluded the 2–3 percent of people who suffer from severe cognitive disabilities (Dweck, 2006). Other authors, such as Geoff Colvin (2008) and Daniel Pink (2005), also support the power of mindset and deliberate practice. Before jumping into the CCSS, it is essential to consider mindset and plan to address it openly. Having a growth mindset will help set the stage and ease the transition to successful implementation of the Common Core.

MEMORIZATION TO RIGOROUS LEARNING: THE SECOND PRONG

The second prong of the approach is developing a plan to explicitly teach thinking skills to all students in all grades. We cannot assume that all children have these skills, given that so many of them have not been required to think, problem solve, read, or write at high levels. For too long, students have gone without explicit instruction in thinking, which has created a gap between what they have been doing in class and what they must be doing in class. This gap must be recognized and bridged if we expect all students to master the Common Core grade-level and anchor standards before graduation.

We must keep in mind that the CCSS will go into effect in nearly all states by 2014. The standards will not just be implemented in kindergarten and then progress upwards as the children move through the system. Rather, they will be implemented K–12 for all students. Therefore, students who heretofore have been learning in systems focused on preparing them for state tests where rigor is questionable will now be learning the Common Core standards without the benefit of starting with them in kindergarten. Of course, younger students will fare much better, but a huge shift will be expected of students already in middle school and high school. These students will come into the Common Core midstream. They have spent the past 10 years learning a test-prep curriculum, so learning new and different ways of thinking will be a challenge. They will be expected to tackle the rigorous learning progressions without having the foundation from elementary school. This will be hard work for students and teachers alike.

The good news is that there is research available to guide us in creating lessons that teach students to think, solve problems, and effectively communicate. The research shows us that the effective starting place is with metacognition. Metacognition is the practice of thinking about thinking. It involves knowing how we learn best and consciously controlling our learning. Teaching students to think about their thinking and their learning process will equip them with the skills and tools they need to manage the CCSS expectations, and the skills are applicable in all content areas and grade levels. As you consider the utility of teaching metacognition to all students, ask these questions: Can your students determine which thinking skills should be used for which tasks? Do they determine what each task entails and purposely choose a strategy to tackle it? Do they regulate their thinking based on how well they are progressing? Do students establish goals for their own learning? Students who are not taught metacognitive skills will lag behind students who do have these skills as they progress to more complex material in the CCSS.

One of the most powerful habits that students with metacognitive skills develop is that they effectively analyze what they have to do, and they do it automatically. They actually engage in self-regulation of their learning. They think about their choices, monitor the effectiveness of their choices, and they set goals for future learning. Exhibit 4.1 shows a comparison of the characteristics of metacognitive learners and nonmetacognitive learners.

Teaching students metacognitive skills helps them accept responsibility for their learning. It helps them develop a growth mindset, and it sets them on a path for success in college and careers. But they cannot learn these strategies without explicit instruction from highly competent teachers.

Comparison of Metacognitive and Nonmetacognitive Learners

Metacognitive Learners	Nonmetacognitive Learners
• Describe their strengths as learners	• Are unaware of their strengths as learners
• Analyze learning tasks to consider options	• Complete learning tasks by rote
• Activate their skills to complete the task	• Have no strategy in choosing skills to complete a task
• Explain their choices in completing learning tasks	• Complete learning tasks without knowing how or being able to explain how
• Monitor the effectiveness of choices during and following the learning activity	• Pay little attention to their choices in learning
• Regularly set goals for learning	• Do not set goals for future learning

The most effective way to teach metacognition is to begin with direct instruction of the levels of thinking from Bloom's *Taxonomy of Educational Objectives* (Bloom, et al., 1956), and the updated Bloom's levels (Anderson, et al., 2001), or from Norman Webb's Depth of Knowledge model (2002). Teachers should explain the levels of thinking and engage students in lessons that require them to compare and contrast, analyze, synthesize, evaluate, judge, defend, etc. The teacher models what thinking sounds like when an analysis is underway. This is commonly called a "think aloud." The teacher talks through the steps the brain follows when a thinking skill is used. Students hear what happens in the brain of a person who is using a skill such as analyzing, evaluating, or synthesizing. They then practice by following the teacher's lead; they share how their thinking progresses as they complete the given task. Practicing doing these kinds of "think alouds," modeled by the teacher, will help make metacognitive skills automatic as students tackle various learning tasks. Students will also learn what thinking strategies work best for them, and they will realize that not everyone will use the same strategy at the same time. Metacognition is highly individual. Teachers can foster metacognition in their students when they ask and/or encourage students to do the following as part of their daily routine (Foster, et al., 2002):

- Explain the learning task in their own words.

- Express what they plan to do before, during, and after the work.

- Consider which of their personal strengths and interests are relevant to completing the task.

- Set goals for future learning based on assessing what worked best this time and what they think they should keep or change.

- Explain what was working through the task and what it taught them about themselves as learners.

John Hattie, researcher and author of *Visible Learning* (2009), a meta-analysis of more than 800 meta-analyses involving millions of students and 15 years of research, found that deliberative practice makes a significant difference in students moving from surface knowledge to deep knowledge. Hattie suggests, "It is not deliberative practice for the sake of repetitive training, but deliberative practice, focused on improving particular aspects of the target performance, to better understand how to monitor, self-regulate, and evaluate their performance, and reduce errors" (p. 30). Students who practice metacognitive thinking as part of their daily routine in all classes will have few problems with the learning progressions in the CCSS, especially when that practice is accompanied by high-quality instructional techniques in literacy and math aligned with the CCSS.

College instructors and employers are in sync when it comes to defining educational rigor and the essential skills of the 21st century. To be college and career ready, students must be able to think critically, solve problems, work in teams, communicate effectively and persuasively, take initiative, and demonstrate persistence in the completion of a project. Educators must transition from the old definition of rigor—right answers—to the rigor required by the Common Core. As stated by Tony Wagner (2008a):

> The rigor that matters most for the 21st century is demonstrated mastery of the core competencies for work, citizenship, and lifelong learning. Studying academic content is the means of developing competencies, instead of being the goal, as it has been traditionally. In today's world, it's no longer how much you know that matters; it's what you can do with what you know.

SUMMARY

The Common Core State Standards are designed to ensure that all American students graduate from high school ready to succeed in college and careers. The standards are internationally benchmarked, and raise the bar on what is expected from our students and when it is expected. Both the English language arts and mathematics standards require that our students solve complex problems, think critically, read and write proficiently, and develop and defend their ideas effectively.

Teaching these rigorous standards will be a daunting task for even our most veteran teachers, especially those educators in states where the current state standards have been deemed "clearly inferior" to the Common Core. Teachers and administrators alike will need support and quality, consistent, job-embedded professional development in order to close the gap between their current teaching practices and the practices needed to move all students to mastery of the Common Core. They will also need quality, rigorous curriculum frameworks to connect the CCSS to units of study and daily learning objectives developed at the district and/or school level.

A high school diploma with good grades and advanced coursework should be a guarantee to parents and students that students have the foundation needed for success in a rigorous academic environment. Students can trust that their K–12 education has been rigorous enough for the challenges of college and careers, and that they will not suffer the fate of the emperor wearing his new suit of clothes.

Key Points

- The United States is seemingly losing its position in the global marketplace to developing countries in the East.

- The impetus for change and increased rigor in the educational system is coming from politicians, business leaders, colleges and universities, and parents.

- The Common Core State Standards have been designed to address this "rigor gap" by establishing learning progressions that require students to read critically, write and speak persuasively, solve problems, and defend opinions in order to prepare students for college and careers.

- Students must be explicitly taught metacognitive skills at the earliest grades and reinforced through graduation to successfully meet the rigors of the Common Core.

- Students who monitor their own learning and regulate their thinking based on the given task develop high-level thinking skills that are transferrable from content area to content area.

- These skills, along with quality content instruction, will propel students to mastery in all content areas.

- Teaching to higher levels of rigor requires two elements:

    1. Students and teachers must develop a growth mindset. They must believe that all students can successfully progress through the standards even if they fall behind, if they are praised for effort, and taught persistence, and have an understanding of how the brain grows as it exercises.

2. Students must be taught metacognitive skills; they must think about their thinking process. This involves having students effectively analyze what they have to do and automatically employ a thinking strategy to complete the task. It also involves having students self-regulate their learning. They must think about their choices, monitor the effectiveness of those choices, and set goals for future learning.

References

Ainsworth, L. (2010). *Rigorous curriculum design: How to create curricular units of study that align standards, instruction, and assessment.* Englewood, CO: Lead + Learn Press.

Anderson, L. W., et al. (2001). *A taxonomy for learning, teaching, and assessing: A revision of Bloom's taxonomy of educational objectives.* New York: Longman.

Bloom, B. S., et al. (1956). *The taxonomy of educational objectives: Handbook I, cognitive domain.* New York: David McKay.

Carmichael, S., Martino, G., Porter-Magee, K., & Wilson, W. (2010). *The state of the state standards—and the Common Core—in 2010.* Washington, DC: Thomas B. Fordham Institute.

Colvin, G. (2008). *Talent is overrated: What really separates world-class performers from everybody else.* New York: Penguin Group.

Common Core State Standards Initiative (CCSSI). (2010, June). *Common Core State Standards for English language arts & literacy in history/social studies, science, and technical subjects* (PDF document). Retrieved from www.corestandards.org/assets/ CCSSI_ELA%20Standards.pdf

Costa, A., & Kallick, B. (2000). *Discovering and exploring habits of mind.* Alexandria, VA: ASCD.

Dweck, C. (2006). *Mindset: The new psychology of success.* New York: Random House.

Foster, G., Sawicki, E., Schaeffer, H., & Zalinski, V. (2002). *I think, therefore I learn!* Ontario: Pembroke.

Friedman, T. (2005). *The world is flat: A brief history of the twenty-first century.* New York: Farrar, Straus and Giroux.

Guggenheim, D. (Director). (2010). *Waiting for Superman.* Paramount Vantage and Participant Media.

Hattie, J. (2009). *Visible learning: A synthesis of over 800 meta-analyses relating to achievement.* New York: Routledge.

Kohn, A. (1999). *The schools our children deserve.* Boston: Houghton Mifflin.

National Commission on Excellence in Education (NCEE). (1983). *A nation at risk: The imperative for educational reform.* Washington, DC: Author.

Pink, D. H. (2005). *A whole new mind: Moving from the information age to the conceptual age.* New York: Penguin.

Resnick, L., & Hall, M. (1998). Learning organizations for sustainable education reform. *Daedalus: The Journal of the American Academy of Arts and Sciences, 127,* 89–118.

Wagner, T. (2008a) *The global achievement gap.* New York. Basic Books.

Wagner, T. (2008b). Rigor redefined. *Educational Leadership, 66*(2), 20–25.

Webb, N. (2002). Depth-of-knowledge levels for four content areas. Wisconsin Center for Education Research. Retrieved June 16, 2011, from http://www.providenceschools.org/media/55488/depth%20of%20knowledge%20guide%20for%20all%20subject%20areas.pdf

Weber, K. (Ed.). (2010). *Waiting for Superman: How we can save America's failing schools.* New York: Perseus Book Group.

Yazzie-Mintz, E. (2010). *Charting the path from engagement to achievement: A report on the 2009 high school survey of student engagement.* Bloomington, IN: Center for Evaluation & Education Policy.

Structures
for Supporting
All Learners

Bonnie Bell

Imagine traveling to a city you never visited. You do not have a road map or a brochure that highlights the city's destinations. You have to get to a particular place by a certain point in time. You wander aimlessly, asking for directions along the way.

That is what going into the classroom without a road map for implementing the Common Core State Standards may be like for some. In order to successfully implement the Common Core for all students, teachers need specific instructional strategies that will assist them in presenting these new concepts and skills. Although the CCSS establish consistent expected achievements, they do not prescribe how teachers should teach and modify their instruction in order for all learners to be successful. In fact, the Common Core may unintentionally create barriers to learning for some students if teachers attempt to use traditional delivery models for these new rigorous standards.

So how can teachers and educational leaders provide instructional supports for students to ensure that *all* learners can access these rigorous standards? What are the systemic structures that can be put into place to close the academic achievement gap? Two strategies that can help teachers successfully implement the CCSS are structured lesson design and interventions.

STRUCTURED LESSON DESIGN

When teachers are asked what resource is the most precious to them, the inevitable answer (even before money) is *time*. Teachers cannot create additional time within the instructional day; however, creative practitioners most certainly can control the way time is used. Successful teachers systematically and carefully plan for productive use of instructional time. One way of using time efficiently is through thoughtful decision making about the organization of a lesson and the strategies that will be employed to master the Common Core.

The most important strategy to improve student achievement is to ensure that the initial presentation of content in the classroom, or "first instruction," is strategically crafted and systematically taught. In other words, fortifying regular classroom instruction is essential to supporting all learners, prior to the implementation of any interventions. The teacher is the most essential factor that determines student success. Various research-based methodologies for lesson design are utilized in classrooms across the nation, including *Universal Design for Learning* (Metcalf, 2011); *Explicit Direct Instruction* (Hollingsworth and Ybarra, 2009); *Direct Interactive Instruction* (Action Learning Systems, 2011); and *Working on the Work* (Schlechty, 2002). These blueprints for lesson design share several key elements. Educators should employ the CCSS in ways that are consistent with these widely accepted best practices or frameworks that guide educational practices so that instruction will be developed in ways that provide all students with a full and fair opportunity to meet the standards.

Element 1: Learning Objectives

Why is the learning objective the most essential part of structured lesson design? The Common Core State Standards explicitly describe what students should know or be able to do (that they couldn't do before). The standards are the new learning, and as such, need to be dissected in order for teachers to truly understand the concept attainment and skill level needed for student mastery. "Unwrapping" standards is a proven methodology for providing this instructional clarity. When teachers take the time to analyze each standard and identify its essential concepts and skills, the result is more effective instructional planning, assessment, and student learning (Ainsworth, 2003). Just like any other standard, the Common Core State Standards need to be "unwrapped" in order to reveal the concepts and skills.

Once a teacher has "unwrapped" the Common Core standards, the stanards will need to be transformed into "kid-friendly" terminology. Objectives need to be stated or written for every instructional exercise. Presenting students with kid-friendly objectives and making them readily available so students can see and understand the objective at any given moment provides them with a purpose for learning—it gives students a clear picture of what the outcomes for the class period are supposed to be and what is expected of them as learners. Furthermore, clearly identifying the objective guides the instructor during the planning process and with the selection of learning activities. Research by John Hollingsworth and Silvia Ybarra (2009) and their methodology of *Explicit Direct Instruction* suggest that teachers state objectives in behavioral terms for students. For example:

> Given (state the condition under which the students will perform the objective), the students will (state an observable student behavior) with (state the criteria here—a statement that specifies how well the student must perform the behavior) accuracy. An example of a behavioral objective is: "Given an unlabeled diagram of the solar system, the students will label the nine planets and the sun with 80 percent accuracy."

"Unwrapping" the standard and then explicitly stating the content objectives are essential first steps for any instructional lesson. Teachers and students must truly understand the level of concept attainment to ensure that the rigor of the Common Core State Standards will be met. Maintaining rigor is key to the success of all students, especially those at risk.

Element 2: Instructional Classroom Routines

A systematic process for classroom procedures is another critical part of successful structured lesson design. Most educators give forethought to daily classroom management routines such as taking attendance, transitioning, turning in completed assignments, and what to do when finished with work, but instructional routines are equally important to predict and design. For pedagogical reasons, instructional procedures are essential to ensuring that teaching and learning is as engaging as possible. And research supports the need for functional routines as part of the lesson design. Vallecorsa, DeBettencourt, and Zigmond (2000) found that instructional classroom routines positively affect students' academic performance, as well as their behavior.

Teachers must incorporate explicit procedures into their daily operations for how students should respond during the learning process, including: consistent cueing systems for getting students' attention, cooperative learning routines, interactive routines for participating in a discussion or responding to the teacher, and so on. Just like administrative or managerial routines, instructional routines must be explicitly taught and modeled for students and taught in situational settings. These skills, too, need to be reviewed and practiced frequently until they are internalized and become habits for learning.

Designing effective instructional procedures not only creates a smooth-running classroom, but also produces a more pleasant experience for teachers and students alike. More importantly, instructional classroom routines make it possible for students to learn more efficiently and more effectively (Classroom-Management-Success.org, 2011). Students shouldn't have to figure out on their own what they should and should not be doing during a lesson. The benefit of establishing effective classroom routines is additional time for instruction, practice, and reteaching of the CCSS—a luxurious resource for any teacher!

Element 3: Organization for Concept Development

Sequentially organizing the lesson is an art. The beauty of a lesson lies in how it unfolds, so that it not only enables students to acquire learning, but also engages students in the learning process itself. Just like artists, educators have a palette and various instruments or tools with which to work. The canvas comes alive as the facilitator of the learning artfully constructs the learning piece by piece. To walk into a classroom and see a teacher just lecturing in the front of the room is not only boring; it is also appalling. This outdated methodology is akin to educational malpractice, because we have research-based tools for lesson design that we know are crucial to concept development, including:

1. **Using anticipatory sets:** Explaining to students why the content in the lesson is important for them to learn.

2. **Continuous scaffolding:** Chunking the learning into small, manageable parts: "I do; We do; You do."

3. **Activating prior knowledge:** Purposefully moving something connected to the new lesson from students' long-term memories into their working memories so they can build upon existing knowledge.

4. **Guided practice:** Working problems with students at the same time, step-by-step, while checking that they execute each step correctly.

5. **Multiple means of engagement:** Providing multiple pathways for students to actually learn the material presented.

6. **Comprehensible input:** Providing clear academic tasks and utilizing multiple modalities to accomplish the assigned task.

7. **Cooperative learning:** Facilitating opportunities for students to work in groups in order to complete tasks collectively.

8. **Utilization of clear and consistent academic language.**

9. **Using multiple means of representation:** Presenting

the content so that it meets the needs of all students, and represents the information in various formats.

10. **Flexible groupings:** Grouping students of varying ages, backgrounds, and abilities and regrouping to meet instructional needs.

A word of caution, however, is needed. Successful practitioners who develop well-designed lessons and are effective at instructing all students do not always adhere to their lessons in lock-step fashion. Such stringency obstructs the teaching and learning process. Detailed preparation must allow for flexibility. Successful teachers, just like successful creative artists, make appropriate judgments about schemata at various points throughout a lesson. Thus, instructors need to make adaptations and add to the artistry of classroom delivery (Honolulu.hawaii.edu, 2011).

Success in implementing the CCSS will require purposeful lesson design. Organizing the delivery of instruction and the sequence of the activities is a thoughtful process. Time taken to incorporate the 10 research-based tools listed above will be instrumental to educators as they organize and create the lessons they will use to address the Common Core.

Element 4: Feedback

"Anybody who's ever been a student knows the difference between getting a paper back stamped with a letter grade and getting it back covered with thoughtful feedback. One may quantify your progress, but the other actually tells you what you did right and how to improve" (Education-Portal.com, 2010). Feedback has a major impact on the success of all learners, and so should have a major influence on lesson design. Hattie and Timperley (2007) state that feedback is one of the most powerful influences on learning and achievement, and that feedback directed at self-regulation and cognitive processes is the most impactful in moving learners toward mastery of nonnegotiable skills. It is essential that students receive feedback in a timely manner and using a precise methodology.

Educators need to ensure that correctives, as well as affirmations, are overtly stated for the work that students perform. In a study released at the Campus Technology 2010 conference, Waypoint Outcomes found that students are more engaged and learn more effectively when they receive consistent feedback. They also found that timeliness, clarity, and personalization are the most important qualities in instructor comments (Education-Portal.com, 2010).

Acknowledging the important role that timely feedback plays as part of structured lesson design assists all learners in moving toward the next benchmark on the continuum of learning the Common Core.

Element 5: Indicators of Success

Every lesson, no matter how short or lengthy, should have a methodology for gauging student success. Teachers must have a way of determining the answer to the question, "I taught it, but did the students get it?" Indicators of success are brief formative assessments that give the instructor the opportunity to evaluate student acquisition of the intended objective. It can be as simple as students holding up whiteboards with their answers, or it can be a three-question, open-ended response to a teacher-initiated prompt. This allows facilitators of learning to check for student understanding of the intended objective, and provides quantitative evidence that learners have mastered the concept and skills of the learning objective. In other words, it indicates that they are ready to either work independently or move forward with additional objectives.

For lengthier lessons, Phillip Schlechty (2002) labels this as "product focus"—the means for students to demonstrate what they have learned. When designing an indicator of success, the needs of English language learners, students with learning disabilities, and students who are "gifted and talented" need to be considered. The creation of multiple pathways to success, choices, novelty and variety, and authentic assignments are inherent in the design of indicators for success. The following two examples from Vulcan Productions' *Success at the Core* (2010) are indicators of success that focus on multiple pathways, choices, and cooperative learning:

Indicator of Success: Multiple Pathways/Choices
Example: English Language Arts

Your class is about to start reading *The Call of the Wild* by Jack London. When you taught this novel last year, you asked students to answer chapter questions as they read. These questions proved to be ineffectual. The questions did not challenge your strongest students. Many students got bored and stopped paying attention as they used the same process in chapter after chapter. This year, you decide to try a new approach. You create choice boards for three segments of the book (Chapters 1–3, Chapters 4–5, and Chapters 6–7). Each choice board has four rigorous activities linked to the chapters. Each student must complete one of the activities after the class finishes reading the chapters. By the end of the book, all students will complete three activities. Choices include: writing a letter to the author, creating a dialogue between two characters, penning a book review, and making a scrapbook that captures what happens in the chapters. You work with students one-on-one to help them select assignments that are appropriate to their level and learning needs.

Indicator of Success: Cooperative Groups

Example: Mathematics

Your students work in cooperative learning groups to review their homework and complete in-class assignments. For homework review, students choose their own groups. Most often, they pick peers who share similar interests or are involved in the same out-of-school activities. As a result, each group includes students with a range of math skills. Using an established small-group protocol, you ask students to go over the previous night's homework. When students work on in-class assignments, you group them by ability. You form groups using standardized test scores, as well as formative and summative assessments. Students work through problems with peers at their same level. This means that during small groups you provide focused help to lower-level groups and enrichment work to groups who excel. This flexible grouping method removes the stigmas that may arise if student groups are formed solely based on ability.

Equally important for students to know is how formative assessments will be measured. Product standards in the form of a rubric, and an example of what a proficient product looks like, are crucial. Schlechty (2001) found that students are more likely to persevere with the learning when the standards by which a project or product will be judged are clear. "When problems, issues, products, performances, or exhibitions are a part of the instructional design, students understand the standards by which the results of their work will be evaluated. Furthermore, they are committed to these standards, see them as fair, and see a real prospect of meeting these standards if they work diligently at the tasks assigned or encouraged" (p. 115).

Structured lesson design involves much more than making arbitrary decisions about what to teach each day. It is a multifaceted and intricate process. It is an art. Practitioners that develop systematic, thoughtful plans based on research-based characteristics reduce the barriers to implementing the Common Core. They provide *all* learners with appropriate access, resources, and assistance, while also maintaining the rigor of the intended objective. Employing these vital lesson features will allow not only regular education students but also special populations and students at risk to thrive in school by being able to master the Common Core.

INTERVENTIONS

Schools that emphasize characteristics of structured lesson design provide for tailored instruction that meets the needs of most students to master standards. However, when good first instruction fails, then additional instructional strategies must be implemented in order for students to have every opportunity for success.

Once we can ensure that first instruction is as effective as it can be for students, and academic achievement gaps are still occurring, then instructional supports for students who have still not achieved proficiency on the standards must be provided. Providing students with ample opportunities to gain nonnegotiable skills and concepts is the key to any successful program. When students receive the support they need, their confidence grows and schools become places where all students can succeed. But, how do we design support structures that help all students succeed?

The Response to Intervention movement has swept across the nation over the past few years with great force, due to the fact that educators have long recognized that removing students from regular instruction to receive separate services has not made a huge impact on the achievement gap problem. In some instances, pulling kids out of regular classrooms has had negative consequences and has even created gaping holes in achievement due to the fact that students who are removed from classroom instruction inevitably miss something, so instructional coherence is lost. Those students are also perceived by their peers as being different.

Response to Intervention provides a model that allows for students to overcome academic deficiencies by providing early, effective assistance to children who are having difficulty learning. It is designed to function as an early intervention tool in order to prevent academic failure. When good first instruction does not meet the academic needs of a student, then the school provides for supplemental instruction. Core instruction is still delivered by the classroom teacher, with the addition of targeted instruction for 30 minutes per day, two to four times per week for a minimum of nine weeks.

If students are still not making appropriate progress, then

more intense, explicit instruction will be warranted. Students will then need to be part of specially designed instruction either in the regular education setting by replacing the core content area materials with materials that are specifically designed for intensive interventions or through specialized services.

As part of any intervention program, regular assessment to measure student mastery of nonnegotiable standards is essential—especially for at-risk students. Periodic common formative assessments are essential to diagnosing and monitoring student progress toward mastery of the CCSS. Regular assessments are useful in giving teachers vital information for grouping and reteaching of necessary skills. Formative assessment that focuses on small improvements also serves as a motivational tool. Both teachers and students can witness incremental improvements.

SUMMARY

As our nation prepares for the implementation of the Common Core, we must shift our systemic traditional model of education in order to provide for richer learning experiences, so that all students can access the rigorous CCSS. For the last 100 years, educational practices have focused on skills-based instruction, in which the teacher is the dispenser of knowledge. Partnerships of authority and professional learning communities, in which teachers work in collaborative Data Teams, will be essential elements to ensuring that practitioners can become facilitators of the Common Core, providing students with meaningful learning activities to access these rigorous contents and skills. The CCSS will serve as an important guide for teachers to ensure they are preparing students for college and the workforce.

However, the implementation of the Common Core alone will not be enough. Learning for all students must be enhanced though well-developed, content-rich lessons that are complemented by the five elements of structured lesson design, and through purposeful interventions.

The five elements of structured lesson design are:

1. **Learning Objectives:** Educators must "unwrap" the CCSS to fully understand each standard, and then must make the learning objective of each lesson available to students in kid-friendly language.

2. **Instructional Classroom Routines:** Just as teachers have specific procedures for taking attendance and turning in homework, they should also implement specific instructional procedures, such as consistent cueing systems for getting students' attention, cooperative learning routines, and interactive routines for participating in a discussion or responding to the teacher.

3. **Organization for Concept Development:** Carefully organized lessons unfold in a way that enhances both student learning and student engagement in the learning process. Ten research-based tools should be considered when designing each lesson: Using anticipatory sets, continuous scaffolding, activating prior knowledge, guided practice, multiple means of engagement, comprehensible input, cooperative learning, utilization of clear and consistent academic language, using multiple means of representation, and flexible groupings.

4. **Feedback:** Thoughtful, relevant, timely feedback is important to the success of all learners.

5. **Indicators of Success:** Each lesson should incorporate a method for gauging student success. Novelty, variety, authenticity, and the inclusion of multiple pathways to success should be taken into account when designing success indicators.

When good first instruction isn't enough to bring all students to proficiency on the CCSS, interventions must be implemented. The Response to Intervention model provides methodology that enables students to overcome academic difficulties.

References

Action Learning Systems. (2011). *Direct interactive instruction (DII): As powerful as one-on-one tutoring.* Retrieved March 12, 2011, from www.actionlearningsystems.com/index.php?q=content/ direct-interactive-instruction-dii-powerful-one-one-tutoring-0

Ainsworth, L. (2003). *"Unwrapping" the standards: A simple process to make standards manageable.* Englewood, CO: Lead + Learn Press.

Allington, R. L., & Walmsley, S. A. (1995). *No quick fix: Rethinking literacy programs in America's elementary schools.* New York: Teachers College Press.

Classroom-Management-Success.org. (2011). *Consistent classroom routines: Practice makes permanent.* Retrieved March 13, 2011, from www.classroom-management-success.org/classroom-routines.html

Colvin, G., & Lazar, M. (1995). Establishing classroom routines. *The Oregon Conference Monograph, 7,* 209–212.

Education-Portal.com. (2010). *Study finds that classroom feedback encourages student satisfaction and effective learning.* Retrieved March 13, 2011, from education-portal.com/articles/Study_Finds _That_Classroom_Feedback_Encourages_Student_Satisfaction _and_Effective_Learning.html

Hattie, J., & Timperley, H. (2007). The power of feedback. *Review of Educational Research, 77*(1), 88–112.

Hollingsworth, J., & Ybarra, S. (2009). *Explicit direct instruction (EDI): The power of the well-crafted, well-taught lesson.* Thousand Oaks, CA: Corwin.

Honolulu.hawaii.edu. (2011). *Lesson planning procedures* (Original source and date unknown). Retrieved March 12, 2011, from honolulu.hawaii.edu/intranet/committees/FacDevCom/guidebk/teachtip/lesspln1.htm

Metcalf, D. J. (2011). *Succeeding in the inclusive classroom: K–12 lesson plans using universal design for learning.* Los Angeles, CA: Sage.

Ogle, D. M. (1997). *Critical issue: Rethinking learning for students at risk.* Retrieved February 21, 2011, from www.ncrel.org/sdrs/areas/issues/students/atrisk/at700.htm

Schlechty, P. C. (2001). *Shaking up the schoolhouse: How to support and sustain educational innovation.* San Francisco, CA: Jossey-Bass.

Schlechty, P. C. (2002). *Working on the work: An action plan for teachers, principals, and superintendents.* San Francisco, CA: Jossey-Bass.

Vallecorsa, A. L., DeBettencourt, L. U., & Zigmond, N. (2000). *Students with mild disabilities in general education settings: A guide for special educators.* Saddle River, NJ: Prentice Hall.

Vulcan Productions. (2010). "Support structures to help all middle school students succeed." *Success at the core: How teams of teachers transform instruction.* Retrieved March 10, 2011, from www.successatthecore.com/artifacts/QI_Elements_Support Structures_FINAL.pdf

Effectively Implementing the 100-Day Action Plan

Stephen Ventura

Because of the rapid adoption of the Common Core State Standards, many schools, districts, and state education departments must now form steps to properly implement these new educational standards. They must be able to monitor actions and resources, provide technical support for teaching and learning, and identify the instructional and assessment resources that are currently in hand that align well to the new standards, and those that do not, just to name a few.

Each organization can accomplish these tasks, but it may be beneficial to create a set of specific steps, accompanied by a specific timeline for implementation, to use as a guideline. The use of 100-day action plans can help manage the transition from a state's current set of standards to the Common Core. A 100-day CCSS action plan is not meant to be a comprehensive checklist of all the issues that your organization will need to consider as it moves from adoption of the CCSS to implementation. More precisely, it is meant to be a preliminary step to begin the necessary discussions and tasks required for successful Common Core implementation. It is important to realize that not everything you need to accomplish can be completed within your first 100 days;

however, your action plan should focus on making the greatest difference well beyond 100 days.

With Kentucky leading the way, the vast majority of states have now voluntarily chosen to adopt the CCSS (as of April 25, 2011). Many states adopted the CCSS in their entirety, with the option of adding an additional 15 percent from their existing English language arts and math state standards. Additionally, there are varying degrees of support from state departments. Some state departments, including the Kentucky Department of Education, have provided resources to assist with statewide implementation. These resources include a crosswalk that demonstrates the alignment of the CCSS, the standards used to develop the Kentucky Core Academic Standards, and the current Kentucky standards (available at www.education.ky.gov). There are also drafts of deconstructed, or "unwrapped," Kentucky Core Academic Standards in language arts and mathematics. Both of these resources are worth replicating, as they will help teachers, schools, and districts create courses and units of study. If your state department has not yet begun to provide additional resources for implementation, don't wait. Your 100-day CCSS action plan can help close the implementation gap by providing a clear and focused progression towards district-wide reform.

The Common Core requires new levels of rigor and specificity, so it is imperative that schools and districts sequence and organize an implementation timeline to ensure parity and uniformity.

100-DAY ACTION PLANS

There is no single authority on how to create a 100-day action plan. The following suggestions form a simple guideline to follow when creating your own 100-day action plan. I have used these guidelines to implement grading policies, curricular and leadership decisions, and technical changes to an entire organization. Even the best educational action plans will fail if they are poorly implemented, and will ultimately have little opportunity for impact. The suggestions presented here are designed to assist education agencies faced with crucial decisions about CCSS adoption.

FIVE STEPS TO A 100-DAY ACTION PLAN

To create a 100-day CCSS implementation/action plan, first select a policy or strategy that could make the greatest difference in your organization if you accomplish it. Identify why this particular strategy really matters over the long haul for all stakeholders. What will the accomplishment of this strategy really mean in terms of motivation, achievement, and professional practice?

You can quickly organize your plan by considering the following five steps:

1. **Select a project or projects that will have the greatest impact on student achievement.** For example, if your organization started creating and implementing common formative assessments based on power standards, how would this impact your current reality? What difference would common formative assessment of power standards make in achievement?

   It is important to address the current number of Common Core standards, particularly in English language arts, where the totals in each grade level are considerable. Factor in that individual states have the option of including 15 percent of their existing state standards along with the CCSS, and you have the potential of running out of instructional days. Mike Schmoker, in his new book *Focus* (2011), estimates that schools using the CCSS will only be able to effectively teach *half* of them in the time available on a typical 180-day instructional calendar. Power standards may be a strategy worth implementing because of instructional time constraints.

You may also consider addressing the increasingly complex writing expectations of the CCSS, in all subjects, facilitated by all teachers. How could social studies, science, and math teachers add more writing to their instruction?

Formative assessments, power standards, and writing expectations are just a few suggestions that can help jump-start CCSS implementation, and that can therefore serve as the focus of your 100-day action plan.

2. **Identify in advance when you will measure and report on indicators that show short-term wins.** Populate those actions first on your 100-day action plan. Remember, short-term wins lead to long-term impact.

3. **Once you have your actions for measuring and reporting on indicators in place, fill in with other high-powered actions.** Use the LEAD tool to help you do this:

   Learning: Actions that require you and others to learn.

   Evidence: Actions that require you to collect, analyze, and use data to guide decisions.

   Attitude: Actions that challenge unhelpful attitudes

(yours and others') and that support emotions and attitudes that help the project.

Decisions: Actions that put you at a decision point.

4. **Build in actions that require you to learn and try new, helpful leadership behaviors as you roll out your project.** Look for ways to overcome your personal leadership Achilles' heel. In an article that appeared in *Educational Leadership* (2007), Doug Reeves suggested that leaders need to "emphasize effectiveness, not popularity." Too many change efforts fail because leaders have underestimated the power of the prevailing culture to undermine change. To challenge that culture, leaders must be prepared to stand up for effective practices, even if those changes are initially unpopular.

Teachers in every school know right now which students are in danger of failure at the end of the year, and they know that with immediate intervention and extra time, many of those failures could be avoided. Yet one of the least popular actions any teacher or school leader can take is to change a student's schedule or curriculum during the year. It is easier to wait for failure at the end of the year and use the same practices in the following year, all the while hoping for different results. If the litmus test for goal achievement is the short-term popularity of the changes necessary to implement the goals, then the strategy is doomed. Change inevitably represents risk, loss, and fear, a triumvirate never associated with popularity.

5. **Update your project weekly.** Your 100-day action plan allows you to premeditate the most powerful actions

needed to move your project forward in the first 100 days. Review and revise these actions promptly and as needed. Do not let a week go by without doing this. It is critical that your phase-in strategies and timelines are updated on a regular and frequent basis.

Have you ever visited a favorite Web site looking for new information, only to discover that the site has not been updated in months? No matter how many times you check, the same information is presented. How likely is it that you will keep visiting that site? You probably determined that the site has been abandoned, since there is no evidence of new information. The same is true with action plans. Lack of updates and timely feedback could equate to zero interest.

COMMON MISTAKES

While creating your 100-day action plan, try to avoid the six most common mistakes associated with action planning:

1. **Organization:** Lack of a winning strategy, or inability to implement that strategy.

2. **Role:** Failing to align expectations and resources or key stakeholders.

3. **Personal:** Gaps in individuals' strengths and/or motivation.

4. **Relationship:** Failing to establish and/or maintain key relationships up, across, or down.

5. **Delivery:** Failing to build a high-performing team and deliver results fast enough.

6. **Adjustment:** Not seeing or not reacting to situational changes.

Effective action plans invite implementation; however, there is one misconception called "buy-in," a term frequently used when we launch new initiatives. Doug Reeves, founder of The Leadership and Learning Center, stated it best when he said far too many organizations rely on the "vision, buy-in, action" formula. Instead, Reeves believes that the correct formula is "vision, action, buy-in" (2011). The rationale is simple: How can stakeholders buy into any high-impact initiative if they don't see it in action and see the results of those actions? This is especially critical with a CCSS action plan. Just talking about standards isn't enough. Many of us have been through standards implementation before. But the CCSS provide unprecedented opportunities for sharing resources across the country, emphasizing literacy on a number of interdisciplinary levels, and providing students with a level playing field complete with consistent exposure to higher levels of rigor.

If your plan doesn't get you to start something right away, then it probably isn't worth the time and effort of even beginning the process. According to The Leadership and Learning Center's national research, you are most likely to implement changes if they take place within 100 days from the time you consider them. Although some changes may take many years to accomplish in full, you should begin by focusing on changes that you can make immediately, within the next 100 days.

PLANNING, IMPLEMENTING, AND MONITORING THE COMMON CORE ACTION PLAN

With guidance provided by The Leadership and Learning Center, an implementation and monitoring plan for the CCSS was developed that was presented to all Kentucky state superintendents. This thoughtful and comprehensive organization of key practices provides a foundation for meaningful action.

As seen in the implementation and monitoring plan shown in Exhibit 6.1, Kentucky is planning to monitor 11 high-impact initiatives to support CCSS implementation:

1. Communication
2. Initiative Inventory
3. Learning Context
4. Professional Development
5. Curriculum Design
6. Quality Instruction
7. Access and Acceleration
8. Assessment Inventory
9. Effective Feedback
10. Accountability
11. Systemic Alignment

This list seems all encompassing, so perhaps there are ways to provide additional focus without compromising intent. Schools and districts can sometimes lose their ability to focus if there are too many priorities.

BOOK ONE
EXHIBIT 6.1

Kentucky Implementation and Monitoring Plan

Implementing and Monitoring the Kentucky Core Academic Standards

District/ School	Implementation Plan	Activities/ Timeline	Assignments/ Resources
Communication	**Develop strategic communication plan for staff, students, parents, the community:** • Ensure clear, consistent messaging regarding KCAS. • Engage all stakeholders. • Help develop a solid understanding of KCAS by providing access to available resources (local, state, national). • Publish district "road map" for implementation.		
Initiative Inventory	**Align current initiatives with KCAS:** • Identify district-/school-wide initiatives and programs. • Assess rigor of initiatives and programs with KCAS. • Assess fidelity to intended implementation model. • "Weed the garden" as needed (remove ineffective programs).		
Learning Context	**Assess and consider rethinking:** • Staffing patterns. • School schedules. • Course design and pathways for college and career readiness. • Instructional materials and resources. • Technology. • Structure for collaboration.		
Professional Development	**Consider needs for professional development in these areas:** • Effective Data Teams. • Sufficient depth in content expertise. • Literacy across content areas. • Creating exemplars for grade-level expectations and progressions. • Increasing nonfiction writing across the curriculum.		

WHAT WOULD THESE SAY ABOUT WHAT OF THESE HAD THE MOST IMPACT

Kentucky Implementation and Monitoring Plan *(continued)*

District/ School	Implementation Plan	Activities/ Timeline	Assignments/ Resources
Professional Development *(continued)*	**Consider needs for professional development in these areas:** • Developing an understanding of mathematical practices and their connection to context. • Increasing levels of rigor and thinking strategies. • Differentiating instruction. • Assessment literacy. • Creating performance assessments. • Incorporating engaging qualities in instruction and in student tasks. • Other, as determined by district.		
Curriculum Design	**Build the foundation:** • Establish learning progressions for standards, clustering, or bundling standards when appropriate. • Develop curriculum maps. • Revise pacing guides. • Select and/or construct unit planning organizer. **Design units of study:** • Review deconstructed standards and create student-friendly learning targets. • Review model lessons and units. • Create unit assessments (pre-assessments, post-assessments, and progress monitoring checks). • Ensure that weekly and daily plans for instruction follow the written curriculum implementation plan. • Design formative assessment, including performance-based assessments and tasks.		

Kentucky Implementation and Monitoring Plan *(continued)*

District/ School	Implementation Plan	Activities/ Timeline	Assignments/ Resources
Quality Instruction	**Implement standards-based instructional practices:** • Focus on clearly defined standards. • Implement engaging learning experiences provided in student-centered classrooms. • Engage student thinking through effective questioning. • Provide student tasks to promote higher levels of thinking. • Conduct frequent formative assessments to monitor learning, refine instruction, and plan intervention.		
Access and Acceleration	**Ensure differentiation:** • Design structures and strategies for access and acceleration for all subgroups, including English language learners, students with Individualized Education Programs, and gifted students. • Organize the Response to Intervention model to maximize all school resources, including human resources.		
Assessment Inventory	**Create a balanced assessment program:** • Ensure alignment of current assessments with the KCAS, noting inconsistencies and gaps. • Consider implications of online assessments. • Understand status and growth metrics.		

BOOK ONE EXHIBIT 6.1

Kentucky Implementation and Monitoring Plan *(continued)*

District/ School	Monitoring Plan	Activities/ Timeline	Assignments/ Resources
Effective Feedback	**Utilize feedback strategies that advance learning for students and teachers:** • Utilize Professional Learning Communities as Data Teams to monitor progress and respond to the effectiveness of instruction. • Ensure teachers understand effective feedback strategies as a critical part of formative assessment. • Utilize rubrics to identify levels of success, including student-developed rubrics. • Examine and consider revising grading practices. • Promote students self-assessing their own progress toward the learning targets; utilize student-led conferences.		
Accountability	**Incorporate new measures into a holistic accountability system:** • Monitor what is valued. • Examine cause data (adult actions) and effect data (student results). • Promote lateral accountability through a collaborative process to design, teach, reflect, and revise. • Act upon the evidence. • Celebrate successes.		
Systemic Alignment	**Ensure KCAS alignment with:** • The school and/or district improvement plan. • Supervision and evaluation policies and practices. • Assessment policies and practices. • Funding sources. • Systemic focus of time, effort, and resources.		

Planning

Many state departments of education have stated that the CCSS cannot be "powered." In other words, their position is that there are fewer standards in the CCSS documents than in many standards systems, and all of them are essential and deserve the same amount of instructional focus. Even if we accept that the CCSS are adequately focused, enabling teachers to cover all of them without any prioritization, the assumption is that students need to gain only one year of learning to achieve those standards. But in my experience as a professional developer, many of the schools I serve have students who need *more than one year of learning* to achieve proficiency. And if the CCSS are more rigorous than previously established state standards, then even more students will need more than one year of learning in order to achieve grade-level proficiency. That means schools have to do one of three things:

1. Extend the length of the school day and instructional year so teachers have more time to address more than one year of learning objectives;

2. Accept that many students, particularly the economically disadvantaged, will not achieve a year of growth; or

3. Understand that some standards are more important than others and give schools the ability to "power" the standards.

Until we discover that frantic coverage of everything leads to better achievement, prioritizing the standards may be the most realistic option.

If you are working in a state or region that believes in perfect coverage of all standards, then you may want to audit other current initiatives and determine their educational impact. Two guiding questions can be used to determine the effectiveness of initiatives:

1. Are we really using it? —How Do You Know?

2. Is there strong evidence that it is directly related to improving student performance? —How Do You Know?

To give credibility to teachers, we must be willing to eliminate practices that don't meet the criteria in the questions listed above. This is especially critical if you work in an environment where "everything is important." Figuring out where each educational strategy in the school or district falls on Doug Reeves' initiative matrix (Exhibit 1.1, in Chapter One) can help educators determine which initiatives should be given more attention and which should be weeded out.

Implementation

It will be essential for all stakeholders to investigate the content of the CCSS. It will not be possible to take a passive stance as your state transitions to new learning requirements. For the deepest implementation, teachers and leaders must participate in meaningful professional development so that the implications of the standards can be fully understood. All personnel, including superintendents, board members, teachers, and leaders, must understand the means of implementation of the CCSS, and how they will affect what is already being done. Practitioners must continue to study how to meet the needs of all learners, as well as how these standards will affect policy and leadership.

Monitoring

To provide effective feedback for any high-impact initiative or action plan, there must be an accountability and alignment system that monitors adult actions, not just test scores or other outcome data (Reeves, 2011). You must decide on what you are going to monitor and measure, because the critical variable for any action plan is deep implementation. You simply cannot manage what you do not measure. Monitoring your CCSS action plan ensures regular observation of adult actions. Brian McNulty and Laura Besser (2011) say that the biggest mistake that people make in leading change is not creating enough of a sense of urgency. Therefore, your CCSS action plan must be focused on something that is wildly important. Action plans can empower adults with a sense of conviction, because the scope of work to be completed

BOOK ONE EXHIBIT 6.2   **Action Plan Resource/Personnel Assignment**

Timeline	Big Ideas/ Key Elements	District Actions	District Focus	Who	Resource Materials
2011–2012	Support Resources for CCSS Orientation	• Provide district-wide awareness of ELA and mathematics CCSS • Focus professional development on instructional practices	Introduction to the CCSS and instructional practices	• Core District Leadership Team • Site-based leaders	Support resources for professional development

really matters. To accomplish this, make sure your plan includes, in addition to activities and timelines, needed resources and persons responsible (see Exhibit 6.2).

LEADERS AND THE CCSS ACTION PLAN

As you discover the tactical elements that will have the greatest impact in helping to implement the CCSS, remember to:

1. Specify the actions needed to address each of the top CCSS issues.

2. Develop an overall action plan that depicts how each goal will be reached.

3. Develop a plan for each major function of the CCSS, e.g., personnel, resources, and support.

4. Ensure that all stakeholders have a copy of the CCSS action plan.

5. Specify the goals to be accomplished and how each goal contributes to the entire organization.

During the 2011 Super Bowl championship game, where was Green Bay Packers head coach Mike McCarthy? What was he doing? If you said he was on the sideline coaching his team, you are correct. Can you imagine what might have happened if he stayed in his office during the Super Bowl? What might have been the reaction from the fans and players? It seems obvious that the Super Bowl is an important event that requires all of his attention.

The same questions should be asked of educational leaders. Where are they during important parts of the instructional day?

Why do district superintendents and principals spend a majority of their time on management rather than instructional leadership? Why aren't they coaching from the sideline while their "players" teach? Higher levels of leadership focus are associated with greater gains in student learning (Reeves, 2011).

Action plans are merely words on paper unless they get you to start doing something. They are lists of adult actions that should be taken in order to achieve a desired end result. To make the leap to better action planning and implementation of the CCSS, leaders must be able to get in front of the game, not wait passively for the state to tell them what to do. Even though states hold the key to better implementation of the CCSS, we can still reflect on our own personal experiences with previous standards adoption. What do you know now about standards implementation that you didn't know back in the 1990s when a majority of educators experienced their first encounter with educational standards? What would you do differently this time (see Exhibit 6.3)?

It is one thing to set goals, but an entirely different thing to *get* goals. Use your 100-day action plan to share a powerful vision and develop a clear plan for the achievement of that vision. In fact, once your plan is complete, display it on your district Web site, conduct informational community meetings, and build the capacity of the plan with other educators and school systems in your area. We are becoming a nation of networked educators working with the same set of educational goals and standards. It makes sense to create networked action plans for deeper and more consistent application of the Common Core.

BOOK ONE EXHIBIT 6.3

Lessons Learned from Standards Implementation

Recall when your state or local school system implemented standards-based reform. What were the most and least successful leadership efforts? Examples are listed below.

	Most Successful	Least Successful
The moral case for standards against the bell curve.		
Implementation of standards-based assessments.		
Implementation of standards-based grading.		
Narrowing the focus of standards-based curriculum.		
Other instructional leadership grading initiatives or standards.		

SUMMARY

- 100-day action plans can be organized using five simple steps:

  1. Select project(s) that will have the greatest impact on student achievement.

  2. Identify what you will measure and monitor.

  3. Look at actions that require *all* to learn: students, teachers, and leaders.

4. Implement the best leadership behaviors.

5. Update and maintain your plan.

- A 100-day action plan can assist with planning, implementing, and monitoring of the CCSS, especially if you focus on certain aspects of the Common Core that will make a big difference in your organization if you achieve them.

- Not everything in your plan can be accomplished within the first 100 days of implementation; however, your action plan should focus on actions that will make the greatest difference and that will have effects that last well beyond 100 days.

- You are most likely to implement changes if they take place within 100 days from the time you consider them. Although some CCSS changes may take many years to accomplish in full, you should first focus on changes that you can make immediately, within the next 100 days.

- Leaders must audit current initiatives and decide if the range of implementation is having an effect on student achievement. Implementation audits can help make time for deeper Common Core implementation, which requires a considerable degree of organization and time.

References

Bradt, G., Check, J., & Pedraza, J. (2006). *The new leader's 100-day action plan.* Hoboken, NJ: Wiley & Sons.

McNulty, B., & Besser, L. (2011). *Leaders make it happen: An administrator's guide to data teams.* Englewood, CO: Lead + Learn Press.

Reeves, D. B. (2007, March). Closing the implementation gap. *Educational Leadership, 64*(6), 85–86.

Reeves, D. B. (2011). *Finding your leadership focus: What matters most for student results.* New York: Teachers College Press.

Schmoker, M. (2011). *Focus: Elevating the essentials to radically improve student learning.* Alexandria, VA: ASCD.

Index

Academic difficulties, overcoming, 122, 125
Access, 17, 80, 90; acceleration and, 134
Accountability, 17–18, 24, 25, 134, 141
Achievement, 129, 139, 143; gaps in, 74, 86, 111, 122; goals for, 131; improving, 15, 16, 24; initiatives and, 16; learning and, 118; projects for, 129–130; student, 2, 4, 10, 13, 90, 112, 144; technology and, 17
ACT. *See* American College Testing
Action Learning Systems, 113
Actions: high-power, 130; leadership behaviors and, 131, 145; literacy, 70, 83; monitoring, 127
Ainsworth, Larry: on rigorous curriculum, 97
American Association of School Administrators, 64
American College Testing (ACT), 62, 81
Analysis, 90, 95–96, 104–105, 108
Andersen, Hans Christian, 89
Anticipatory sets, using, 116
Arguments, 38–39, 95
Assessments, 12, 24, 33, 55, 97, 134; ACT, 62; collaboration on, 10; effective, 113; norm-referenced, 3; planning for, 54; resources for, 127; standards-based, 18; systems, 4; writing and, 8. *See also* Formative assessments; Summative assessments
Avatars, 80

Balance, 2; accounting for, 17–18
Baltimore Sun, 66
Behavior, 2; intelligent, 100; leadership, 131, 145; student, 114
Bell, Bonnie, xiii

Bell curve, 3, 4, 5, 7
Besser, Laura, 141
Best practices, implementing, 55, 57
Black holes, 69, 70
Bloom, Benjamin, 100, 103
Books, online, 59–60
Brain, growth of, 107
Building blocks, 46, 56
Buy-in, 133

Call of the Wild, The (London), 119
Campus Technology 2010 conference, 118
CCR. *See* College and career readiness
CCSSI. *See* Common Core State Standards Initiative
CCSSM. *See* Common Core for State Standards for Mathematics
Cell phones, 80, 81
Challenges, 10–11, 18, 70–71
Change, 7; impetus for, 107; implementing, 145; popularity of, 131; situational, 133; social, 72; sustainable, 19; technical, 129; transformational, 67; undermining, 131
Change Leadership Group, 90
Children's Internet Protection Act, 73
Citizen journalists, 67; adolescents as, 78, 80–83, 84 (exh.); literacy and, 81; standards for, 84 (exh.); technology and, 80–81; thinking/communicating like, 85 (exh.)
Citizenship, 65, 92, 105
Classrooms: routines in, 114–115, 124; standardization of, 20
Clusters, 49, 53
Code of ethics, 83
Cognitive disabilities, 100
Cognitive processes, 118

Domains, 53; mathematics, 49, 50
  (exh.), 51 (exh.)
Dropouts, 17, 93
Dweck, Carol: mindset and, 99–100

Economic problems, 12–13, 70, 72
Education: decisions on, 64; spending
  on, 90, 92–93
Education Week, 3
Educational Leadership (Reeves), 131
Eisenhower, Dwight D., 72
ELA. *See* English language arts
Emperor's New Clothes (Andersen),
  analogy to, 89–90
Engagement, 17, 116
English as a second language, 5
English language arts (ELA), 14, 24, 27,
  30, 40, 129; CCSS for, xiv, 23, 26,
  33, 36, 43, 44, 53–57, 65, 66, 67–
  68, 69, 75, 78, 79 (exh.), 86, 92, 94;
  Kentucky Core Academic
  Standards in, 128; language
  standards and, 42; success in, 119;
  writing and, 39
Entrepreneurialism, 90–91
Evaluate, described, 15
Evaluation, 12, 90, 104
Expectations, 48, 81, 86, 132;
  connections and, 74–75, 78;
  literacy, 64–69; resources and, 132;
  skills and, 102; standards and, 43–
  44; writing, 130
Explicit Direct Instruction
  (Hollingsworth and Ybarra), 112,
  114

Facebook, 60
Failure, consequence of, 6, 131
Feedback, 3, 6, 12, 97; effective, 117–
  118, 124, 132, 134, 141
Focus (Schmoker), 130
Formative assessments, xiv, 120, 123,
  129, 130; challenges of, 10–11;
  measuring, 121
Franklin, Christina, 72–73
Friedman, Thomas, 4, 91

Gibbs, Robert, 64
Gifted and talented, 119
Gladwell, Malcolm, 64
Global Achievement Gap, The
  (Wagner), 90
Global economy, 24, 78, 107
Goals, 142; communication of, 61;
  setting, 108, 143
Grading policies, 129
Groups: flexible, 117; working in, 91
Growth, 31, 75, 107; achieving, 139;
  incremental, 100; monitoring, 86

Habits of Mind (Costa and Kallick), 99–
  100
Hall, Megan Williams, 100
Hattie, John, 104–105, 118
Health, physical education and, 17
Health care, literacy and, 65
High School Survey of Student
  Engagement, 93
History: CCSS for, 53–57; literacy in,
  26, 35–36, 39–40; reading standard
  3 for, 37 (exh.); writing standard 7
  for, 40 (exh.)
Hollingsworth, John: research by, 112,
  113–114
Hope, promise and, 23–24
Horizontal articulation, 54
Huffington Post, The: on citizen
  journalists, 83

"I do; We do; You do," 116
Ideas: communication of, 61; knowledge and, 31; presentation of, 41
Impact, measurement of, 15, 16
Implementation, 1–2, 13, 19, 23, 26,
  101, 112, 117, 123, 128, 129, 132,
  134, 140, 141, 142, 143, 145;
  checking, 9–12; lessons learned
  from, 144 (exh.); successful, 14;
  timeline for, 127
Implementation Audit, 13, 14–15, 19
Improvements, 123
Indicators, measuring/reporting on,
  130